TEAM
MEMBER'S
SURVIVAL GUIDE

Jill A. George, Ph.D., and Jeanne M. Wilson

McGraw-Hill

New York   San Francisco   Washington, D.C.   Auckland   Bogotá
Caracas   Lisbon   London   Madrid   Mexico City   Milan
Montreal   New Delhi   San Juan   Singapore
Sydney   Tokyo   Toronto

McGraw-Hill

A Division of The McGraw-Hill Companies

2 3 4 5 6 7 8 9 0   QPD/QPD   9 0 2 1 0 9 8

ISBN 0-07-024566-5

Printed and bound by Quebecor/Dubuque.

Team Member's Survival Guide
Table of Contents

Introduction

Today many organizations are making the transition to teams as a means to improve their efficiency and the quality of work life for employees. The goal is admirable, but the course taken is choppy: The term "team" is ill-defined, leaving employees and supervisors confused. Team in one part of the organization can mean something different in another part.

The irony is that most organizations don't intentionally place this burden on employees. Unfortunately, most organizations don't have the expertise or the time to make a successful, smooth transition to teams. Instead, they often launch into teams without the necessary planning, design, and training. The result can be chaotic. Even though organizations might have a vision for teams, they lack the how-to s.

That's why this guide is designed as a self-coaching tool. It takes you through what you need to do month by month to make your shift to teams as successful as possible. It sets you up for success and helps you evaluate your progress.

This book is written directly to employees who are becoming or who already are high-performance team members in self-directed teams, semi-permanent project teams, and empowered natural work teams. It doesn't matter whether you're a team member in a team of executives or a team of operators, whether you work in a service or a manufacturing organization—this guide is designed for you.

Mapping the Voyage

Most teams will go through three distinct phases in their development: Preteam, New Team, and Mature Team.

Preteam Phase

This phase begins when the organization first considers teams. It ends when teams are formally chartered and have held their first meeting. This first phase can last from 4 to 12 months. At the beginning of the Preteam Phase, leaders and employees hold their first discussions about empowered teams. By the end of this phase, everyone has a vision of what teams can accomplish, and you'll have a design for how teams will operate to turn that vision into a reality.

New Team Phase

The New Team Phase begins with the first team meeting and ends about 12 to 18 months later. In the beginning of this phase, you will spend a great deal of time getting your team started by developing a team purpose (or mission) statement, goals, and clear roles and responsibilities. Shortly after start-up, you will spend up to 15 percent of your time making decisions formerly left to management, such as scheduling vacations, assigning daily tasks, and monitoring results. By the end of this phase, you might be working on projects for the team, ranging from increasing involvement with larger business issues to more technical projects.

Mature Team Phase

If your teams have been operating continuously for 12 months or more and are handling most of their new responsibilities successfully, you probably are in the Mature Team Phase. Certain key skills and behaviors distinguish mature teams from new teams: handling new responsibilities competently, solving interpersonal problems, working together willingly, and maintaining predictable levels of high performance. If these skills and behaviors are absent, your teams have not graduated to the Mature Team Phase.

Getting Your Bearings

This survey is designed to help you establish where you are in your team implementation. Are you in the Preteam Phase? The New Team Phase? Somewhere in the Mature Team Phase? To find out, complete the survey by checking the boxes for those statements that apply to your situation.

Preteam Phase

You are in the Preteam Phase if you're:

☐ Becoming aware of the need to change.

☐ Completing a readiness assessment to determine your organization's cultural strengths and developmental areas.

☐ Defining organizational values to drive behaviors toward a more empowered culture.

☐ Still not sure that teams will work.

☐ Responding to skeptics who are wary of the team concept.

☐ Unsure about what your new role will be.

☐ Reconfiguring roles and responsibilities at all levels so people have more decision-making ability.

☐ Redesigning departmental boundaries so teams can control errors or variances within their own boundaries.

☐ Focusing on your personal needs and role.

If six or more of these statements apply to you, you're probably in the Preteam Phase. Pages 1 through 55 will be particularly helpful as you form teams. However, if you think you are beyond the Preteam Phase, you still might want to skim the activities to see if there is anything your team should do to become even stronger.

New Team Phase

You are in the New Team Phase if you're:

☐ Working together with members from different areas or departments.

☐ Making more decisions as a team according to an Empowerment Schedule.

☐ Developing team goals in alignment with your organization's vision and values.

☐ Struggling not to revert to the comfort of your old role, especially during crises or when faced with technically complex problems.

☐ Spending time with your former supervisor to gain more expertise.

☐ Seeing attitudes and behaviors becoming aligned with the team concept.

☐ Receiving more information about customer complaints, profitability, and related business matters.

☐ Focusing more on your teams' needs and roles than on your own needs and role.

As a rule, you're in the New Team Phase if six or more of these items apply to you. Pages 57 through 155 will help you move successfully into the next phase: Mature Teams.

Mature Team Phase

If your teams have been operating continuously for 12 to 18 months and are handling most of their new responsibilities successfully, you're probably in the Mature Team Phase. You are in the Mature Team Phase if you're:

☐ Spending up to 80 percent of your time on strategic customer or product and service improvements.

☐ Working with teams that handle their new responsibilities successfully.

☐ Assuming more advanced responsibilities, such as budgeting, peer review, and salary increases.

☐ Watching your team produce at peak levels.

☐ Maintaining quality levels at an all-time high.

☐ Noticing that doubts about the team concept have practically disappeared.

☐ Stretching to take on roles outside your department or facility.

You've made it to the Mature Team Phase if at least five of these items apply to you. Pages 157 through 187 will help you maintain your high-performance teams.

The Journey

This book is designed to be a user-friendly, month-by-month planning guide to help you successfully navigate through each of the three team implementation phases.

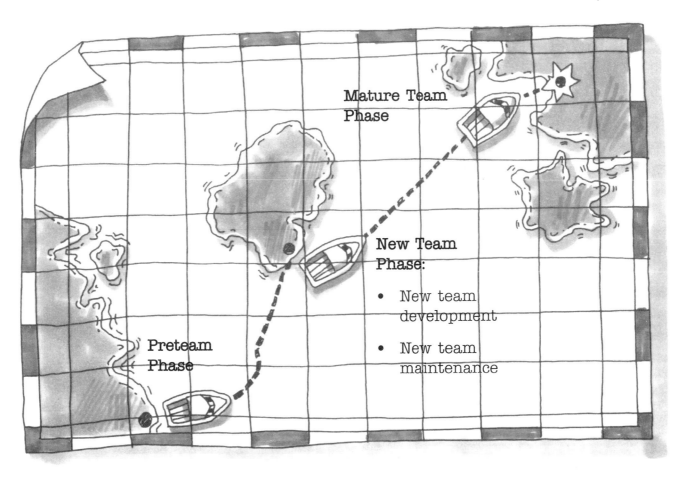

Mature Team
Phase

New Team
Phase:

- New team
  development

- New team
  maintenance

Preteam
Phase

How to Use This Guide

The *Team Member's Survival Guide* is the do-it-yourself reference tool that can help solve your tough team problems. Although the guide is laid out sequentially, we recognize that different teams need to focus on different activities. For this reason we suggest that you browse through the following common team problems and issues to more quickly pinpoint where you need to look for help.

Trust

Trust is the absolute starting place for a team. If you're having trust-related problems, start with yourself first. The chapters Getting in Sync with Your Organization's Direction and Assessing Your Readiness for High-Performance Work Teams will help you understand some of your own trust issues. You also could debrief the readiness assessment (page 47) as a team and discuss the lower scores that seem trust related. The team chartering chapter (page 76) is a good first source for addressing your trust issues. By experiencing the chartering process, many teams can clarify concerns and roles, and set ground rules that build trust.

Keeping Expectations in Line

First, review all the What to Expect sections that appear in the Preteam (page 2), New Team Development (page 58), New Team Maintenance (page 108), and Mature Team (page 158) phases. These sections will outline what to expect and address some of your concerns. Next, refer to the Team Survival Tips sections (pages 22, 60, 110, and 164) for more detail. You can use the tips to calibrate your expectations or use them with your team.

Getting Focus and Keeping It

Teams that are well grounded from the start produce better results than teams that flounder. If your team seems confused about why they are working together or what they are trying to accomplish, start with the chapters that explain the types of teams and the results they achieve (Preteam Month 1, page 4) and how teams fit in with company strategies (Preteam Month 2, page 14). Make sure everyone is on the same page with definitions of teams in your organization. Next, go to the chapter on chartering teams (New Team Month 3, page 76). If your team already has a charter but is still confused, this chapter can clear up things. Teams often spend a lot of time fine-tuning a charter to reach consistent understanding.

Once your team matures, you'll be looking at the organization differently (Mature Team Month 1, page 160)—you'll be looking at the business as a whole to make "big picture" improvements. Then, once you've broadened that focus, you'll learn how to maintain it in Mature Team Month 5 (page 180).

Breaking Down Functional "Silos" Internally or Externally

The *Team Member's Survival Guide* explains several ways to attack functional walls, silos, elevator shafts, or whatever your organization calls department boundaries that can impede your efforts to complete your work on time and within specifications. Start with Preteam Month 5 (page 36) to learn about the tools that organizational-design professionals use to improve collaboration among departments and increase productivity and efficiency. Then apply the tools described in Mature Team Month 4 (page 176) and New Team Month 9 (page 124). As you make more progress, either with internal or external customers, use the tools described in New Team

Month 10 (page 132). Arrange meetings among departments using the tools described in these chapters—and watch those walls come tumbling down!

Your Supervisor's Role

The following chapters in the *Team Member's Survival Guide* can help your team understand how your supervisor's role will change: New Team Month 5 (page 90), New Team Month 8 (page 116), Mature Team Month 3 (page 170), and the *Team Leader's Survival Guide*.

The Skills You Need

Again, all the What to Expect sections in the Preteam (page 2), New Team Development (page 58), New Team Maintenance (page 108), and Mature Team (page 158) phases give you an idea of how you and your job will change. Also, the Team Survival Tips sections (pages 22, 60, 110, and 164) provide additional details on what you'll need to do to succeed in a team-based environment. Preteam Month 6 (page 46) will measure your readiness in the critical team skill areas. New Team Month 1 (page 60) is the main section that lists skills and describes the types of training you'll need.

Keeping Teams Energized for the Long Haul

One of the toughest issues teams face is how to stay fresh and not burn out. Start with the stamina check in New Team Month 10 (page 132). One thing that seems to challenge and energize teams is more face-to-face contact and problem solving with customers. New Team Month 9 (page 124) and New Team Month 10 (page 132) can help you prepare for more exciting work with your customers. Mature Team Month 5 (page 180) offers tips for staying fresh and focused.

Celebrating Success

Mature Team Month 5 (page 180) provides a number of tips on how to celebrate all aspects of your team's accomplishments, from shining results and technical improvements to team development and external recognition.

On Your Own

After you pinpoint where your team wants to go on the Team Development Continuum (page 15), you'll want to skim through the entire guide. This will give you an idea of what to expect and will help you recognize when you or your team is grappling with an issue that is covered elsewhere in the guide. Many team members find it helpful to work on some activities alone. This allows them to focus on self-improvement first, making it easier to work with team members later.

As a Team

Some organizations used an early version of this guide as the weekly agenda for team meetings. Each week one team member would take responsibility for leading a discussion of the issue outlined for that week, helping the team apply it to their own situations. You, too, can follow this format or adopt some other method that best addresses your situation.

Many teams set aside a specific time each week to work through that week's prescribed issues, exercises, and activities. In most cases this review will take about half an hour.

Notes. . .

Preteam Phase

Welcome to the Preteam Phase! The following pages will help you become familiar with (and start addressing) some of the important issues you and other team members will face in the transition to teams. Here is a month-by-month look at the Preteam Phase:

Month 1

Work Teams: A Common Element in Organizational Change

Month 2

Why Are Work Teams Integral to Organizational Change?

Month 3

Team Survival Tips

Month 4

Getting in Sync with Your Organization's Direction

Month 5

Redesign for Results

Month 6

Assessing Your Readiness for High-Performance Work Teams

Preteam Phase

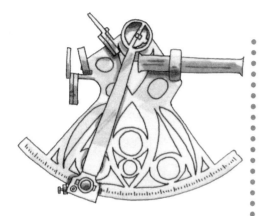

What to Expect

Initial Confusion

In the Preteam Phase people might be confused and in disagreement about the definition of work teams in your organization. Some people think of teams as a temporary fix; others question how far the organization is going with teams or why teams would be a better way to operate. This confusion is common in team implementation efforts—even ones that have been underway for a while! Don't worry too much about this maze of opinions. Discuss the issues and questions and document your conclusions. Once everyone understands where the organization is going with teams, progress becomes easier.

Becoming More Involved

Most likely, you and other people in your organization will spend a lot of time planning how work teams will be set up and how they'll function. You might be asked to participate in meetings to create a vision or a set of values and goals for the "new" organization. Occasionally, you might feel as if this preparation is a waste of your time. Don't let feelings of impatience prevent you from learning from and contributing to the development of the plan for implementing work teams. Failure to plan is one of the major reasons why team implementations fail (Wellins, Byham, and Wilson, 1990). Without substantial employee involvement, effective plans cannot be developed.

Calibrating Your Expectations

Moving to work teams does not always mean that you have the sun in your face and the wind at your back, nor does it translate into "The sky's the limit." Organizations need to establish clearly defined limits, or parameters, that guide employees toward higher levels of empowerment as they learn new skills and gain expertise. Parameters define the "playing field" you have to work within. As a result, the implementation plan will provide a clear route as you start your journey working in teams.

Possible Concerns

> I've been doing my job well for a number of years. I'm not happy with changing my routine at this point in the game.

Fact: Jobs are changing because of increased competition, not because employees have performed inadequately.

It's natural to feel uneasy about a change in your responsibilities. But learning new skills increases your value to the organization and anchors your commitment. The more skills you have, the better you'll be at working a variety of jobs.

> I think most employees can work well in teams. It's the leaders who can't change their spots.

In some situations this is a legitimate concern. Other times, however, it's merely an excuse people use to avoid taking on more responsibility. About 20 percent of all supervisors cannot or will not make the transition to a high-involvement leader. Your job is to be patient and remember that your leaders—like you—are learning to make transitions.

> What about the people in my work area who don't pull their own weight now? How will teams correct that problem?

Teams are certainly not a cure-all for traditional organizations. Certainly many poor performers "come out of the shadows" and take more initiative while working more closely with and becoming more accountable to their fellow employees. However, the deadwood on a team might not respond to newly formed teams. Performance problems are best handled initially by supervisors before teams are officially launched.

What You Will Focus on in the Preteam Phase

- Preparing for Change

- How Work Teams Are a Common Element in Organizational Change

- Team Survival Tips

- Synchronizing Yourself with Your Organization's Direction

- Redesigning for Results: What's It All About?

- Assessing Your Personal Readiness for High Performance/High Involvement

Work Teams: A Common Element in Organizational Change

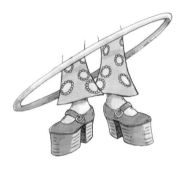

Notes. . .

Are teams a fad? Will some employees rebel while others share the enthusiasm generated by teams? How can you ensure that long after the novelty wears off, teams will continue to be the "in thing"? As you read through Month 1 of your Preteam Phase, you'll learn a brief history of teams (they just didn't arrive on the boat yesterday) as well as the keys to work team success.

History

Empowered teams (often called high-performance work teams) are not new. Permanent work groups that control their day-to-day production, quality, and administrative duties have been getting results since the early 1940s. The equivalent of contemporary work teams was first established in British coal mines. However, it wasn't until the 1970s that work teams started to catch on in North America.

Types of Teams

Teams! Teams! Teams! Everyone is talking teams these days. It seems that just about any group thrown together is called a "team" so organizations can proclaim, "We have teams working on that project." But are the teams in harmony? Probably not. The important thing for you to know is that different types of teams are formed for different purposes to achieve different results. Teams should not be thought of as the result in and of themselves. They are a more effective way of achieving organizational results, not a one-size-fits-all business lifesaver.

The next page illustrates four types of teams. As you can see, the formation of teams is a particular meshing of skills to achieve a defined result, not a rudderless group venturing into unknown territory.

4. Full Speed Ahead

1. Getting Started

3. Getting on Course

2. Going in Circles

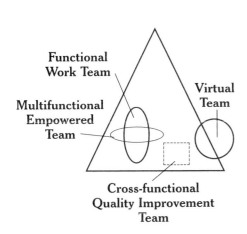

Functional
Work Team

Multifunctional
Empowered
Team

Virtual
Team

Cross-functional
Quality Improvement
Team

Types of Teams

**Cross-functional
Quality Improvement Team**

Functional Work Team

Multifunctional Empowered Team

Virtual Team

Sample Purposes

Gets together for a limited time to recommend solutions to quality problems, either within or between departments, and then disbands.

Works together daily within a functional department to produce high-quality work; leadership is either direct supervision or is shared with an external team leader.

Multiple departments that have been permanently combined or redesigned to eliminate bottlenecks and quality problems from day-to-day work. This team shares a significant number of leadership duties with a leader who provides coaching on tasks as needed and drifts away from direct supervisory responsibilities.

A group of people, possibly from different locations or organizations, charged with reducing day-to-day bottlenecks and errors or reducing cycle time for getting a product or service to market.

The Keys to Work Team Success: How It's Done

Organizations implement change and work teams differently. Some companies follow a top-down approach to implementing teams, meaning that management leads the effort to form teams. Teams in other companies are formed from the "bottom up." These implementations are driven by front-line leaders and employees. Some companies emphasize training to build teams; others, organizational design. What's the best approach?

The following map, which unfolds over the next seven pages, represents our work with hundreds of organizations that implemented teams. This map outlines eight critical steps for a successful teams implementation and details the benefits and potential hazards of each step. The route you choose depends on your needs, but this map should give you a clearer view of how teams are formed and show what each step offers.

Step 1: Establish Clear Organizational Direction

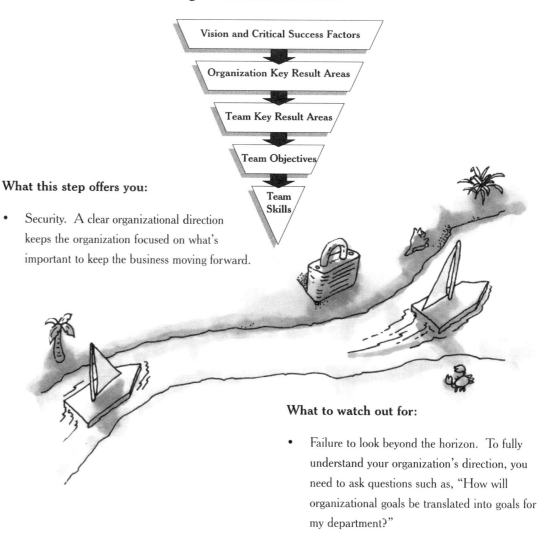

Vision and Critical Success Factors

Organization Key Result Areas

Team Key Result Areas

Team Objectives

Team Skills

What this step offers you:

- Security. A clear organizational direction keeps the organization focused on what's important to keep the business moving forward.

What to watch out for:

- Failure to look beyond the horizon. To fully understand your organization's direction, you need to ask questions such as, "How will organizational goals be translated into goals for my department?"

Support Team

Executives who meet quarterly to revise policies across the organization.

Steering Team

Local site managers who define the vision for teams and gather resources.

Study Group

Groups that develop systems that support the team design.

Design Team

A vertical slice of employees from all areas and levels in the organization who redesign the organization for teams.

Step 2: Encourage Organizational Involvement

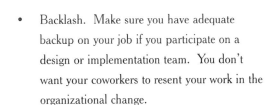

What this step offers you:

- More say. By being more involved, you will be able to identify what's wrong and offer solutions.

- Education. You'll have an opportunity to learn about the techniques in organizational change.

What to watch out for:

- Backlash. Make sure you have adequate backup on your job if you participate on a design or implementation team. You don't want your coworkers to resent your work in the organizational change.

Step 3: Implement Design Principles

Team implementations often use design rules, or principles, for guidance. When these principles are applied, organizations can maximize the work flow and improve the working environment. The following six design principles help organizations achieve their business objectives.

1. Simplicity
2. Cross-training
3. Job ownership
4. Meaningful work
5. Aligned systems
6. Evolution

What this step offers you:

- Guided by these principles, teams produce better results because they're able to correct day-to-day problems themselves without relying on outside sources (Principles 2, 3, and 4). Team members experience more fulfillment because they feel ownership of multiple processes.

- Increased task variety makes your work more interesting and you more valuable to the company.

What to watch out for:

- Bottleneck frustration. Teams designed around single-focused tasks or pieces of equipment rather than ownership of multiple processes cause frustration because the bottlenecks between departments, stations, or support areas remain intact.

Step 4: Phase in More Responsibilities

The following schedule shows how far—and how fast—teams will go. It's a good tool for promoting understanding about teams and clarifying people's expectations about their new responsibilities.

What this step offers you:

- The opportunity to work on more challenging, interesting tasks.

- The chance to prove that you have expertise in leadership tasks.

- The chance to work directly with suppliers, customers, or internal support professionals instead of wasting time going through a swollen hierarchy.

Empowerment Schedule

3 months	6 months	9 months	12 months
• Develop and coordinate a cross-training plan. • Coordinate getting operational safety equipment on the floor. • Handle vacation scheduling. • Assign tasks to members.	• Coordinate time and attendance with human resources. • Run shift overlap meetings. • Review customer feedback as a team.	• Set team goals based on the organization's goals. • Call for materials and maintenance directly.	• Select new team members. • Coordinate the preventive maintenance plan.

What to watch out for:

- Getting in over your head. Take on additional tasks only when you have the skills and information to make accurate decisions. Making decisions without the proper information or training will cause problems and shake your confidence to take on more tasks in the future.

Step 5: Assign Shared Leadership Roles

Shared leadership means ownership and self-direction for the team. For a smooth, orderly transfer of responsibility, there must be a plan.

Organize the responsibilities listed in the Empowerment Schedule (Step 4) by categories or groups of related tasks. These categories will be the points of accountability and contact for team members. Each "star point" is a chance for someone to "own" that responsibility.

In the star point system (see Figure 1), each team member is responsible for a point on the star for a predetermined period. Every three or four months, the star points rotate so everyone has a chance to perform all the functions.

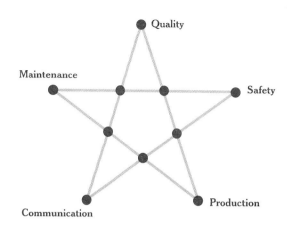

Figure 1

Step 6: Record Team Formation and Charter

The charter should be a formal, typed document to which everyone on the team has easy access. Use a format that best suits your team's needs. Key elements of a charter include:

- Purpose
- Responsibilities
- Completion
- Boundaries
- Ground Rules
- Meetings

What this step offers you:

- Organized accountability among team members.

What this step offers you:

- Clearly defined responsibilities and ground rules that prevent arguments down the road.

What to watch out for:

- Overfilling your plate. Make sure that you have eliminated non-value-adding tasks so that you have time for your new responsibilities.

What to watch out for:

- Lip service. Some team members might not take this seriously—they might just go through the motions.

Step 7: Learn Just-In-Time Team Skills

Team Skills Formula

| Business Skills | X | Job Skills | X | Interaction Skills | X | Team Skills | X | Problem-Solving Skills | = |

Effective Team Performance

What this step offers you:

- Vital skills you need to make more decisions and work with more different people than ever before (customers, suppliers, technical professionals, managers, etc.).

What to watch out for:

- Water on the brain. Too much training all at once reduces your retention. It's like getting hosed down with training. Sessions that are spread out give you a chance to apply skills on the job.

Step 8: Monitor Results

What can teams mean to your organization? The following results prove that teams might have been the catch of the day for these four organizations.

These implementation steps are explained in more detail throughout this guide. So if you aren't realizing the benefit of the steps you've already taken or have overlooked some of these steps, work through this guide. They are tried-and-true and have unleashed some potent results.

Organization	Results
Sandpaper manufacturer	Twenty-five percent greater productivity in redesigned self-directed distribution teams.
Insurance company	A 75 percent improvement in case processing time.
Chemical packaging company	Increased productivity plantwide by 18 percent.
Beer manufacturer	Fifty percent reduction in beer waste.

What this step offers you:

• The *possibility* of team-based compensation when goals are achieved.

• Feedback on your team's progress so you can correct problems and celebrate successes.

What to watch out for:

• Changing tides. You might need to adjust your goals after you receive feedback.

How Do Teams Fit in with Organizational Restructuring?

Restructuring efforts have taken many organizations by storm. A big question people often ask is, "How do teams fit in?" The table on the right reveals answers to this question as it applies to three types of restructuring efforts.

Restructuring Effort	How Teams Fit In
Mergers Two companies combining resources to become one, more competitive organization.	• Employees from different departments of the two companies join forces in teams that can better serve their common customer. • Teams of employees can be formed to create best practices for the new organization.
Reengineering Analyzing the efficiency of major departments, such as billing, bookkeeping, shipping, and marketing, and totally changing how work is done to improve efficiency.	• Teams of employees analyze their work processes. • Natural or multifunctional teams develop new ways to produce their product or service and eliminate inefficient tasks.
Downsizing When the organization lays off employees because it can't financially support their tasks.	• Remaining employees learn to accomplish more with less. • Employees cross-train one another to increase everyone's flexibility and value to the organization.

Why Are Work Teams Integral to Organizational Change?

Month 2

What's Happening in the Change to High Involvement

Things at work seem to be sailing right along. People seem to be getting along reasonably well, and the company is having a good year. But just as you settle in with the status quo, you feel an abrupt lurch—the "t" word, teams, appears on the organization's radar screen, and off course seems to be an inevitable direction. Before you think about bailing out, you, like many others, need to find out: "Why change? Why now?"

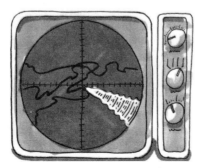

Why Change Now?

- **To increase collaboration and flexibility.**

  Your organization has decided to move toward work teams. You're probably wondering, "Haven't we been working in teams already? Hasn't our good work gotten us where we are today?" You're not alone. Even though the answer to both of these questions might be "Yes," your organization might need even more high-powered, more *consistent* collaboration within and among departments. As one supervisor mentioned, "We thought we had teams all along, but what we really had was *instructed* teams. That is, we cooperated when we were instructed to."

  Many organizations need to expand on their current level of teamwork. When organizations don't use teams to their fullest potential, critical team skills lie dormant.

Consider the Team Development Continuum on the right. Most organizations obtain good results at a "3" or a "4." But work teams are a necessity—they even flourish—in today's competitive environment. It's not uncommon for work teams to operate at a "5," "6," "7," or beyond. In fact, a study of high-involvement practices (Lawler, et al., 1995), shows that 68 percent of corporations use high-involvement work teams.

Where do you think your organization should dock on the Team Development Continuum? If your organization were to receive skills training and employees could make more decisions, where would your organization be in two years?

Now: _____

In two years: _____

Team Development Continuum

Supervisor Centered		**Team Centered**

Area of Supervisory Responsibility

Area of Team Responsibility

1 Supervisor decides and announces decision; employees follow supervisor's directions.

2 Supervisor presents decision, which might change, given employees' comments.

3 Supervisor presents problem, asks employees for ideas, and makes decision.

4 Supervisor/Leader gives feedback and recommendations when team organizes its own work (who does what) or certain aspects of its work.

5 Team handles daily productivity and quality issues, including internal customers and suppliers. Leader handles most personnel functions (training, selecting, appraising) and coaches team members through production and quality issues.

6 Team handles work inputs and outputs, including dealing with external customers/suppliers, selects own team members, schedules own vacations. Leader shares expertise in personnel function areas while transferring other functions to the team.

7 Team is responsible for all personnel functions, including appraisals and compensation. Leader consults with team as needed and spends more time on strategic issues.

Organizations that reach a "5" or "6" on the Team Development Continuum achieve better financial and quality results than organizations at a "4" or lower. A study by John Cotter (1983) revealed these results for organizations with empowered work teams:

- 93 percent improved productivity.

- 86 percent decreased operating costs.

- 86 percent improved quality.

- **To position the organization for the future.**

Organizations change in response to their current financial and market positions and their long-term forecast. Today's nonissues are tomorrow's pressures, and organizations need to change accordingly.

"But our organization is in the highest percentile of quality and speed now. Why change?" you ask. Or you might think the opposite: "Our organization is poised to

head ashore and place a *For Sale* sign out front. We can't afford to change." Both scenarios underscore a basic change tenet: Any company, whether profitable and growing or hemorrhaging and stagnant, can achieve better bottom-line results by using high involvement and work teams.

Do you know your organization's financial condition? Knowing how well your company is staying afloat against a rising tide of increasing costs and competition can give you valuable insight into why change occurs. Ask yourself the following questions and see if the answers put your organization's changes in context.

1. Organizations have to answer to an increasing number of internal and external pressures. Read the list on the next page and compare how your organization responds to each pressure with how the

main competition responds. Write down your comments in the appropriate column. If you don't know the answer, ask your leader.

Internal Business Pressures	Your Company	Competition
Customer Satisfaction		
On-time Delivery		
Quality/Accuracy		
In-house Cycle Time		
Operating Costs		
External Business Pressures		
Market Share		
Geographic/Industry-specific Costs		

2. How will these responses change in five years?

Before answering in the space below, think about this: Can your company afford to operate the same way five years from now? Your company might be the leader of the pack now, but chances are some of your competitors are improving more rapidly. The changes your organization makes now are more likely to secure its future and opportunities for you.

3. What is the impact of the organizational change on you?

    Most people are downright afraid of large-scale organizational change, especially when they lack specific information about what is and isn't changing or how the change will affect their work and career. Before you jump to conclusions, examine both ends of the plank by answering the following two sets of questions.

Part I—Stormy Seas

For this first question, read the example answers to help you think through rationally how the change *could actually affect you*. Then in the spaces provided, answer the question as it applies *to your situation*.

- What is the worst thing that could happen with this change? (Try to provide three alternatives.)

Example	In Your Situation
I'd have to learn how to perform work in other areas of the company.	
I'd have to take on more responsibility.	
I'd have to find work in another organization.	

- Review your answers. In your opinion, what is the likelihood that any of these events would occur?

- If any of the events occurred, would any other opportunities open for you?

Part II—Calm and Clear

For this first question, read the example answers to help you think through rationally how the change *could actually affect you*. Then in the spaces provided, answer the question as it applies *to your situation*.

- What is the best thing that could happen with this change? (Try to provide three alternatives.)

Example	In Your Situation
I'd get to work on a visible project with people from other parts of the company.	
My additional responsibilities would make me more marketable, either in this company or another.	
I'd finally be able to move around to other departments and learn more about the operation instead of being stuck in one area.	

- Review your answers. In your opinion, what is the likelihood that any of these events would occur?

- If any of the events occurred, would any other opportunities open for you?

4. What can you do to make change work in your favor?

Example:

Your first three steps might be:

1) Make a list of things you want to accomplish on a project.

2) Identify your skills that would contribute on a project and inform your supervisor.

3) Tell your supervisor that you are interested in joining a project or design team and explain why you would be an asset.

- Your situation:

- Information you need:

- Who do you need to sell to make this happen?

- Key skills you need to demonstrate:

Notes. . .

Preteam: Team Survival Tips

Notes. . .

Month 3

A major organizational change effort affects everyone. Sure, some team members might want to rock the boat: rejecting every idea, second-guessing all the decisions, and basically creating a one-person mutiny. There are seven key behaviors that can help you survive—and be a winner in—any major organizational change effort. We'll show you how you can use these behaviors to your advantage at each phase in the transition to teams.

Team Survival Tips

1. **Become a quick-change artist.** There's no doubt about it. There's a lot of commotion in the early stages of team implementation. To find the sea of tranquility, keep an open mind to new ideas. People who shoot down ideas from the start are perceived as unable to change. You don't have to blindly accept every idea or change in policy instantly. Just be flexible and give it consideration. Ask

questions; this shows that you're at least considering changes in the organization.

To give you practice in considering new ideas, work through the example on the next page. Whether you consider yourself flexible or not, using this approach to potential changes in your organization will help you think through the benefits of the change as well as show your organization your willingness to consider something new. After completing the example, describe something at your company that's changing. List the potential benefits of the change and how you could see it working.

Example

Change: **The organization is implementing more cross-training within your department and across other departments.**

Potential benefits of this change:

How you could see this change working:

Your Company

Change:

Potential benefits of this change:

How you could see this change working:

2. **Add value.** Most companies, even highly automated ones, need their employees to be more productive. When employees focus on value-adding tasks, their companies have more dynamic and unique approaches to staying ahead of an increasingly crowded fleet of competitors.

Consider how your job can be as fluid as the ebb and flow of the tide. As your customers' needs change, your tasks might need to change as well. The same concept applies to the transition to teams. To be a successful team member during your organization's change, you will need to scope out opportunities to add the most value. Think of your current responsibilities. Are there any that seem needless and need to change? Are there any areas that you haven't explored that would benefit your company? In the space on the right, jot down the tasks you can learn that would add value.

Tasks you can learn that would add value:

Examples might include learning to use a spreadsheet, learning a graphics software package, or creating a troubleshooting guide.

3. Take ownership for yourself and the company. One of the best things you can do for yourself at this early stage of the transition to teams is to think of yourself as your own business—the captain of the ship. As captain, you need to keep your "ship" on course. This means finding ways to improve your skills, rather than waiting to be told what you need to do. One thing you can do immediately is learn more about your company: its competitors, customer service records, long-range plans, market strategy, financial results, and new technology.

You need to take the initiative to build the skills you'll need to succeed in the new team-based organization. After all, you're a big part of the change, and you need to make sure you don't start sinking as you move along the team development course.

Thinking of yourself as your own company, answer the questions in the space on the right. Your responses should give you insight into the key role that being proactive plays in organizational change.

What would you do for yourself if you considered yourself your own company?

Example: **Evaluate how I stack up against the requirements of a team-based organization; define my internal and external customers' expectations.**

What two things could you start on this month?

---

4. **Become a lifelong learner.** In the transition to teams, everyone will learn new approaches to doing their jobs and skills for performing new jobs. Even if your organization doesn't provide you with specific information on your role in teams at this point, it's still a good idea to learn how teams work. Educate yourself on team implementations in your industry. Bookstores, libraries, and the Internet are good resources. Identify an issue or problem that your team is having. Research work teams in other companies to find out how they solved similar problems.

When it comes to teams, your thirst for knowledge should never be fully quenched. In the space on the right, jot down some things you want to learn about teams and how you plan to acquire this information.

Things you would like to know more about concerning teams:

What you plan to do to learn more:

5. **Manage your own morale.** You might have mixed feelings about the move to teams. Occasionally, you might feel good about your new role, doing what the company wants you to do. Other times, you might feel that the change to teams only made things worse and that the company needs to make additional changes, such as in how work gets done and how departments work together. At this stage not everyone will be convinced that the move to teams is good, and they might have negative opinions. Try not to be swayed; maintain your positive feelings. If you feel down, keep track of what's in it for you or think of how the big picture will improve in the long run.

You are in charge of your feelings about your organization's change. It's one thing to say, "When things start going badly, I'll think positive thoughts." It's another thing to do it and take action on those thoughts. Answer the questions in the space on the right and keep them around as a reminder of the importance positive actions play in helping you adjust to changes that affect you.

How can you build on the positive feelings you have about the move to teams and changes your organization is making?

What potential solutions can you develop for problems you complain about?

What's in it (the move to teams) for you?

How will the changes help the organization in the long run?

6. **Monitor your own expectations.** Having unrealistic expectations about the move to teams usually turns into a huge disappointment. Think about it. Is it realistic to expect that you'll be able to make most of the decisions about your work? That you'll have more free time? Or that your supervisor will transform into a team leader superhero overnight? Probably not. Keeping your expectations in check minimizes the disappointments and gives you a balanced perspective when things do fall into place. Two sure-bet expectations in the Preteam Phase are listed below:

- *I expect to be affected by the change.* At least some part of how you work today will be different, and you should be prepared to adjust to the changes before they arrive on your doorstep. You want to be able to ride the waves of change, not swim against the current. Your chances of succeeding in your organization depend greatly on your ability to adjust to new work processes and continuously improve them.

- *I won't know exactly what my job will look like until the New Team Phase.* The New Team Phase begins after teams have been designed and launched—usually a period of five to six months. So keep in mind that when your organization announces it is moving to teams, don't expect to find out all the details about your job.

In the space on the right, list your expectations (both realistic and unrealistic) for your organization's move to teams. List as many or as few as you have and be honest. Then read the suggested tips for dealing with your unrealistic expectations.

Your expectations at this point are:

Realistic

-

-

-

Unrealistic

-

-

-

What you can do to lower your unrealistic expectations and make them realistic:

- Share your expectations with your supervisor. Having this reality check early on with someone who can objectively gauge your expectations and provide additional information can be invaluable.

- Read up on how employees at other team-based organizations managed their expectations.

7. **Yell for what you need.** Do you want more information about why your company is moving to teams and its expected results? Want to find out how other companies are approaching high involvement? What are the plans for teams as they evolve and grow? When organizations move to teams, employees crave information. Unfortunately, when information is not shared, some employees complain silently or outwardly to their peers. This fosters uneasiness about the change, which doesn't do any good for the employees or the company. Tell the right people what you need and want to know. Ask repeatedly if no one follows up with you. Some of the sources you can consult include your leaders, members of design or steering teams, and the human resources department.

There's yelling, and there's *constructive yelling*. Seeking information and getting the answers you need can go a long way toward making you comfortable with a move to teams. Develop an information-seeking plan by answering the questions in the space on the right.

What information do you need to be comfortable with the changes your organization is making?

Where/From whom should you get this information?

Your first three steps for getting what you need are:

1.

2.

3.

Getting in Sync with Your Organization's Direction

Notes. . .

Now that you've had a chance to consider the reasons your organization needs to move toward more empowerment, the big picture should be coming into focus. Your next step is to get in sync with your organization's direction.

What does your organization's direction have to do with you personally? How can you affect it one way or another? Moving to a team-based structure has definite advantages for both you and your organization. The success of the move as well as the speed of the transition depends on how synchronized you and your coworkers are with the direction and transition steps of the company. One of the best things you can do to prepare yourself is to translate the company direction into meaningful direction *for yourself*.

Understanding Your Organization's Strategic Direction

Read through the example on the next page of an insurance company's strategic direction and what it meant to one team member; in other words, how the person translated the direction. Your company's strategic direction might not look exactly like this, but the important thing for you to do is to translate the direction into something that makes sense. Understanding your company's strategic direction will:

- Clear up any confusion about where the company is heading.

- Clarify your opportunities for future growth and satisfaction.

- Help you feel like you're taking an active part in the larger organization.

As you remember from the start of your team journey, the first step for a successful teams implementation is to establish a clear organizational direction. A clear strategic direction typically contains three elements: vision statement, critical success factors, and values/beliefs/operating principles. This example breaks down the insurance company's direction by these elements.

Vision Statement

To be a premier insurance, employee benefits, and financial services organization by:

- Being a partner in the effective, community-based, and integrated delivery of health-management, financing, and administrative systems.
- Providing our customers with superior service and innovative products.
- Valuing an empowered, team-oriented workforce.

What It Meant to One Team Member

"Reading this (the vision statement) helped me understand the importance of alliances with subsidiaries to our future. I need to better understand how to recognize and service subsidiaries. By doing so, I can provide superior service and product knowledge to subscribers."

Critical Success Factors

- Enhance employee effectiveness.
- Improve financial status.
- Exceed customer expectations.
- Expand partnerships.
- Respond quickly to market needs and changes.
- Make best use of technology.

What They Meant to One Team Member

"I can see what the company is focusing on now, and it's different from what we focused on 10 years ago. The critical success factors not only focus on financial goals, but other important areas like employee effectiveness. Working to expand partnerships is part of everyone's job now, not just management's."

Values/Beliefs/Operating Principles

- Customer service
- Quality teamwork
- Open communication
- Care for people
- Long-term focus

What They Meant to One Team Member

"I think if we're going to accomplish the vision and critical success factors, we will need to act slightly differently. For example, now that building partnerships is a part of everyone's job, we're going to have to learn more technical information and collaborate with others who can provide information we need in a way that doesn't delay the customer."

71926

How Would You Translate Your Company's Direction?

Now that you've seen one company's strategic direction, it's time to translate your company's direction into terms that will enhance your understanding of your company's change. Your translation doesn't have to include all the elements from the example.

Vision Statement	What It Means to You

Critical Success Factors	What They Mean to You
•	
•	
•	
•	
•	
•	

Values/Beliefs/Operating Principles	What They Mean to You
•	
•	
•	
•	
•	
•	

A Major Turning Point

By understanding your company's strategic direction, you'll be able to determine how aligned you are with the vision. By aligning yourself with the vision, values, and critical success factors, you'll be able to:

- Determine your performance expectations.

- More readily accept policy changes and changes in work assignments.

- Make suggestions that are more likely to be accepted.

Many people have a difficult time getting in sync with a new organizational direction, especially if they've worked under one set of "rules" for many years. Although there's no guarantee that you'll be 100 percent in sync with all the elements of your company's direction, there are steps you can take to become more aligned with it.

Police Your Synchronicity

Work through the table on pages 33–35 to see how synchronized you are with your organization's direction. Read the examples for each strategic direction element and decide if you are synchronized or not. Then check the appropriate box.

Strategic Direction	You are synchronized if:	You are unsynchronized if:	To become more synchronized, you can:
Vision	• You can see how the work you'll be doing aligns with the vision. ☐ Yes ☐ No	• You'd stand a better chance of understanding hieroglyphics. ☐ Yes ☐ No • You think the vision is totally unrealistic—like something out of a fantasy movie. ☐ Yes ☐ No	• Ask questions to determine how the vision is different from how the company operated before. • Find out the company's plans for implementing the vision. For example, ask managers to explain how the vision can help solve a particular problem.
Critical Success Factors	• Your impression of your company's main goals is that they focus your organization's energy; that is, you believe the company will focus on a few projects and initiatives to achieve the vision, rather than tackling 15 different initiatives at once. ☐ Yes ☐ No	• You believe your company is trying to be all things to all people. In fact, you feel a bit like Carl Sagan felt about stars in the universe: billions and billions of goals. How do you reach them? Nobody knows. ☐ Yes ☐ No	• Ask for examples of how your department's goals link with the organization's critical success factors or goals. • Ask how different department goals link to achieve the vision.

Strategic Direction	You are synchronized if:	You are unsynchronized if:	To become more synchronized, you can:
Values	• The values are consistent with how you normally lead your life in other organizations (sports teams, church groups, etc.). ☐ Yes ☐ No	• You would rather run naked through your organization than live by these values. ☐ Yes ☐ No • You think the values are a joke. No one in management lives these values, why should you? ☐ Yes ☐ No	• Find out what specific steps are planned to support these values. • Ask how feedback will be given about the values.

Strategic Direction	You are synchronized if:	You are unsynchronized if:	To become more synchronized, you can:
Taking on More Responsibility in Teams	• Your initial reaction to the movement on the Team Development Continuum was, "It's about time!" ☐ Yes ☐ No • You and other team members could start immediately on many of the tasks in the Empowerment Schedule. ☐ Yes ☐ No • Your team often takes on more responsibilities without being asked. ☐ Yes ☐ No	• Your initial reaction is that management just wants you to do their job. ☐ Yes ☐ No • You feel the urge to stall the team before they take on additional tasks. ☐ Yes ☐ No	• Prioritize your schedule to accommodate new responsibilities; check with your team leader if adjustments need to be made. • Determine what's in it for you before agreeing to your new tasks. • Consider how your peers will perceive you down the road if you drag your feet. For example, will you be asked to work on interesting assignments in the future?

Well, are you "synching" or swimming with your organization's direction? If you checked three or more "Yes" boxes in the third, unsynchronized column, don't be concerned. Try working on at least two action items that will help you become synchronized with your organization's direction.

Redesign for Results

Notes. . .

Month 5

What Does Redesign Mean?

OK, your organization is moving to teams. Fair's fair: As you're getting used to the idea, you catch wind that your organization is going to restructure and redesign processes. *Restructure? Redesign?*

Don't worry. This is not a tidal wave that will upset your organization's infrastructure. But don't be surprised if you're afraid and confused by the restructuring. Most people experience these feelings for good reason: They don't know what's going to happen or how teams will fit into the new game plan. Even though most organizations restructure for a very good reason—to produce results that will make them more competitive—the idea of going back to the drawing board and redesigning how work could be done more effectively can be threatening. Again, it's OK to feel anxious about this. Hopefully, this chapter will answer your questions about restructuring and help you and your team work more effectively with fewer frustrations.

How Does Redesign Work?

Redesign Tools and How They Might Affect Your Area

Whether redesigning your kitchen or your organization, good tools are the key. Following are three tried-and-true redesign tools that you and your team members can use and will add to your team's success later.

Tool 1

Process Mapping. Imagine you're a patient in a hospital. From the time you're admitted to the time you check out, someone tracks all the staff members with whom you interact, all the tests you take, and all the forms that are filled out. When you leave, you find out that you were moved from one floor to the other and you met 20 different caregivers. Let's take your company. Suppose you followed the development of a product from conception through production, through testing, through final production, to the market. What you would be doing is process mapping. Process mapping tracks all the normal steps in a current process, so you can eliminate the bottlenecks and redundant steps as you redesign.

Tool 2

Analysis of Value-Adding Tasks. Let's return to the hospital. You're wheeled to the radiology department for an X ray. You wait awhile, then find out that radiology wasn't expecting you. So you return to your room, but you know that you'll have to return to radiology for your X ray. Rework for the hospital staff? Frustrating for you? Of course. Analysis of value-adding tasks examines the steps in the process map and determines if they add value to the customer or to keeping the business open. Non-value-adding tasks usually fall into four categories:

- Rework
- Excess movement
- Review
- Excess storage

What kinds of non-value-adding tasks occur in your work process?

- Rework:

- Review:

- Excess movement:

- Excess storage:

Tool 3

Bottleneck Analysis. Aren't delays, backlogs, missed deadlines, and errors frustrating? Errors and backlogs are particularly costly because they lengthen cycle times and lower output. The main purpose of bottleneck analysis is to determine ways to control errors in the process where they start rather than passing them down the "food chain."

When errors are handed off to the next step in the production process, they just get bigger and more costly—they don't disappear! By correcting errors at their entry point—rather than when they sink to the end of the process—you'll actually reduce cycle time and eliminate non-value-adding tasks. In addition, you and other team members will have more control over the quality of your work.

What are the biggest bottlenecks or most common and costly errors in your work process?

Bottlenecks/Errors	How Often They Occur	Costs
•		
•		
•		

Bottlenecks and errors can be controlled at the source in several ways:

- Ensure that each person knows the functions performed before and after him or her in the process.

- Improve the technology so that the bottlenecks are eliminated from the process.

- Put people who have the expertise to solve or control the bottleneck in the same area or on the same team.

Organizations that have effectively redesigned processes use a combination of all three of these methods to control bottlenecks.

If you could minimize or eliminate bottlenecks and errors in your work process, what would it do for you?

[blank response box]

How Redesign Tools Produce Results for You and Your Company

Jobs today aren't meant to stay the same. If they were, people would be racing to jump ship. Even so, when organizations use the redesign tools like those described, people get concerned because their jobs are likely to change to one degree or another. Mistakenly, many employees equate change with downsizing. Even though no one can guarantee employment, employees can maximize their value to their company—and lower their anxiety level—by improving the efficiency of their work processes; in turn, this enhances employees' flexibility to handle different tasks in the future.

Still a bit seasick about more changes? Pull ashore for a few minutes to review the charts on the next few pages, which show how elements of a restructured organization can change and how these changes can affect your work, the organization, and you. There is space in the fourth column for you to add any personal benefits.

Organizational element	How your work changes	Benefits to the company	Benefits to you
Core work process	• Redundant or non-value-adding tasks are minimized or eliminated. • Functional silos are broken down, and employees collaborate on an entire work process instead of isolated parts of the process.	• 50 percent to 200 percent improvement in productivity, cost reductions, customer complaints, and/or cycle time. • Increased knowledge of the big picture required to produce a product or service. • More career opportunities for employees.	• Improves the efficiency of work processes, thereby increasing a person's flexibility to handle different tasks in the future. • • •
Physical facilities	• Equipment and people are moved around to eliminate excess movement or communication bottlenecks due to physical distance. • Status symbols, such as designated parking places, are eliminated. • Meeting space/computers are located at the point of production or service.	• Coordinating work is simplified when everyone needed is close at hand. • Resources the team needs (materials, equipment, etc.) are right at the team's fingertips.	• No more walking two miles in the facility to get the necessary information! • • •

Organizational element	How your work changes	Benefits to the company	Benefits to you
Cross-training of many types of skills	• Skills in which other team members can become proficient within three to six months are identified. • Skills are plotted on a matrix and checked off as team members acquire new skills. • New skill acquisition is linked to team goals and rewards and recognition.	• More interesting work for team members of any profession. • Opportunities for people to learn new tasks. • More flexible employees can assist during busy periods.	• Increases skill level without having to attend school. • Increases value in the marketplace.
Support work processes	• Subdepartments within support departments, such as finance, maintenance, information systems, or the lab, may be placed on the core team.	• Expedites work that must be coordinated among departments. • Less frustration and finger-pointing between departments. • More variety in the work departments can do. • Better appreciation of what is required to perform support and functional tasks.	• Reducing the finger-pointing and blaming makes it easier to get information— no more stonewalling by different departments.

Organizational element	How your work changes	Benefits to the company	Benefits to you
Layers of management	• Managers should be more visible and involved on major projects rather than giving directions. • Tasks and decision making, formerly handled by managers, are given to teams. Teams receive the information and training necessary to take on their new responsibilities. • New responsibilities given to teams are coordinated through functional points of contact on the team.	• Employees have more control and ownership of their work. • Decisions are made much more quickly. • Managers' work is more interesting.	• The perception that managers at different levels perform redundant tasks gradually disappears. Managers involved in different tasks makes it easier to get answers. • • • •
Information systems	• Data that used to be produced by a department is now produced by the team.	• Information like cost reports and customer feedback is more specific and is delivered to the team quickly.	• Reports are more timely and contain accurate, updated information. •

Organizational element	How your work changes	Benefits to the company	Benefits to you
Human resource systems	• Performance management (goal setting and review) is done as a team. • Team members often are involved in selecting other team members or managers.	• Effective team behavior is reinforced over time. • Team goals are aligned with critical organizational goals. • Team members learn key decision-making skills that directly affect their work. These skills, previously reserved for managers, include setting goals for the team and making presentations to upper management.	• Because performance management is done as a team, team members have a stake in one another's performance. • • • •

Getting Involved with Restructuring

As you can see, the changes listed in the charts involve people at all levels of the organization. They also highlight the importance of team members in the restructuring. Successfully implementing these types of changes and realizing the organizational and personal benefits relies on involving people at the point of service delivery—nonmanagement—in the redesign. Team members who are involved early on are more committed to and more likely to succeed in the new environment. The next chapter highlights several ways you can get involved that will increase your value in the organization.

No one ever said change was easy, particularly the people directly involved with redesigning and implementing the change. Your involvement is critical to your and your company's success.

But be prepared to join other hands on deck (peers and leaders) in some of the most challenging work you'll tackle—changing the status quo and making tough but necessary changes that will move the company forward.

So, why *should* you get involved in your organization's redesign? What's in it for the *company*? What's in it for *you*?

Benefits to Your Company

More Accurate Information on the Current State of the Work Processes

When was the last time your boss knew exactly how to do the jobs in your area? Usually, leaders have a snapshot of the overall business but don't know the day-to-day details. That's why employees must be involved in redesign efforts. The more employees are involved, the more complete and accurate the data is on exactly where bottlenecks are in the processes and just how damaging they are to your customers.

A Formula for Successful Teams

Lack of involvement =
Longer implementation time =
Obsolete design =
Behind the competition

Despite looking simple on the surface, this formula sends a critical message: Despite managers' best efforts to come up with a redesign that would send efficiency through the roof, the plan can flop if employees don't understand the rationale for the change or doubt the merit of the design ideas. Organizations that redesign need to inform employees and seek their input. After all, the goal is to have employees jump in—not jump ship—to implement the solutions. As the formula shows, companies that don't involve their employees throughout the redesign effort risk more than just stranded employees who are hesitant or unwilling to commit to the redesign.

Benefits to You

Increases Your Ability to Adjust

Knowing exactly *why* your organization is changing, *when* those changes are likely to take place, and *what* will be changed will better prepare you mentally for what will happen in the future and the adjustments you and others will have to make. By getting involved early on, you will learn the specific steps and plans for the change firsthand and have the facts to counter rumors.

Builds Your Knowledge of the Organization's "Inner Workings"

Knowledge is key to your future job success. The more you know about how all the departments in your company operate and the bottlenecks they regularly have to deal with, the better equipped you'll be to do your job better. And the more flexible you'll be to assist these departments. In addition, you'll have the opportunity to work with people you might not normally work with.

Builds Your Knowledge of Tools for Your Future Use

When you get involved in restructuring, you learn how to use the tools described earlier (process mapping, bottleneck analysis) to analyze data and make recommendations. These redesign tools also come in handy for solving problems on your team or in your area. The better you are at solving specific bottlenecks or work coordination problems in your area, the more control you'll have over your work.

Assessing Your Readiness for High-Performance Work Teams

Notes. . .

Month 6

Wouldn't it be great to know in advance how ready you'll be when the waves of change roll into your organization? Many of these changes probably will affect you in some shape or form. But can you accept them, including a new role and responsibilities, or will you be stuck high and dry while your organization moves forward?

To find out if you're ready, take a few minutes to complete the following assessment. Read the statement(s) under each readiness factor, then circle the number that corresponds to the response that best describes your feelings. There are no right or wrong answers.

After you finish, get your score by following the steps on page 52. Your scores will tell you if you've got your high-performance sea legs or if you need to map out an improvement plan. The table on page 53 can guide you toward developing an effective action plan.

Personal Readiness Assessment for Organizational Redesign

Readiness Factor: Increased Decision Making

I'm able to assume more responsibility and decision-making authority than I currently have.

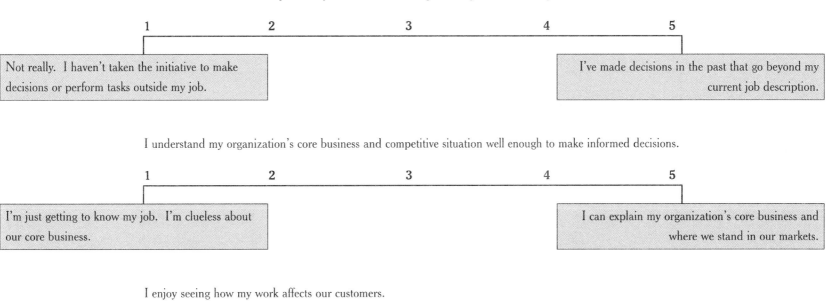

1	2	3	4	5

Not really. I haven't taken the initiative to make decisions or perform tasks outside my job.

I've made decisions in the past that go beyond my current job description.

I understand my organization's core business and competitive situation well enough to make informed decisions.

1	2	3	4	5

I'm just getting to know my job. I'm clueless about our core business.

I can explain my organization's core business and where we stand in our markets.

I enjoy seeing how my work affects our customers.

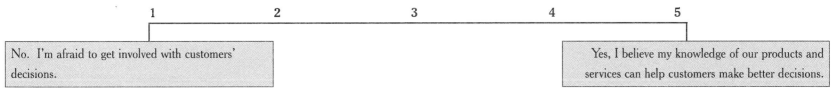

1	2	3	4	5

No. I'm afraid to get involved with customers' decisions.

Yes, I believe my knowledge of our products and services can help customers make better decisions.

Readiness Factor: Working with Support Groups

I'm prepared and willing to collaborate and share work with various support groups to complete a job.

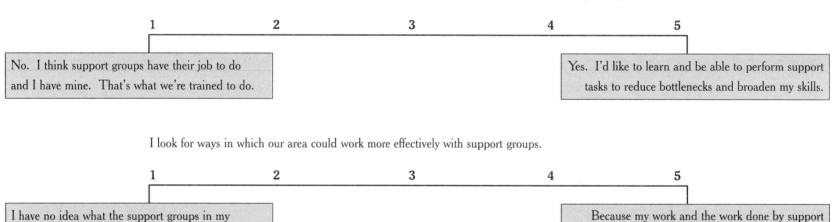

| 1 | 2 | 3 | 4 | 5 |

No. I think support groups have their job to do and I have mine. That's what we're trained to do.

Yes. I'd like to learn and be able to perform support tasks to reduce bottlenecks and broaden my skills.

I look for ways in which our area could work more effectively with support groups.

| 1 | 2 | 3 | 4 | 5 |

I have no idea what the support groups in my organization do.

Because my work and the work done by support groups is interdependent, I know the importance of looking for ways to work better together.

Readiness Factor: Willingness to Cross-Train

The members of my work group teach each other about our jobs in case we need to fill in for someone.

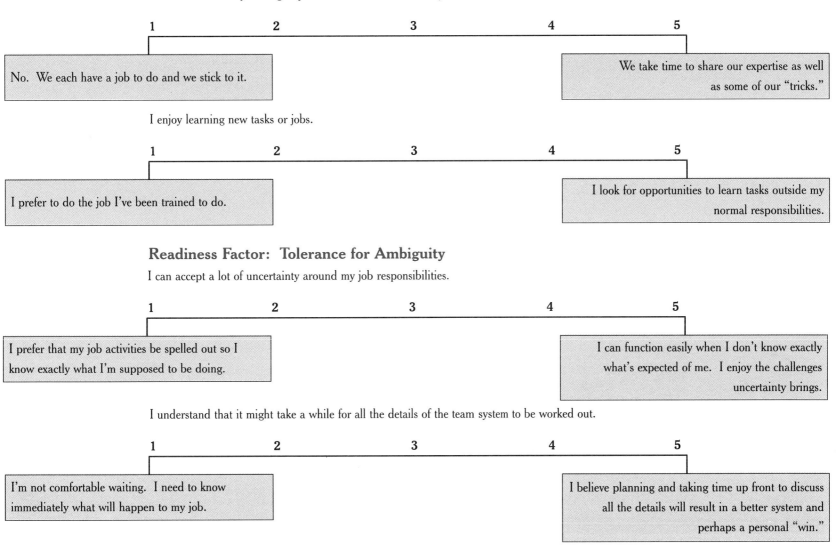

| 1 | 2 | 3 | 4 | 5 |

No. We each have a job to do and we stick to it.

We take time to share our expertise as well as some of our "tricks."

I enjoy learning new tasks or jobs.

| 1 | 2 | 3 | 4 | 5 |

I prefer to do the job I've been trained to do.

I look for opportunities to learn tasks outside my normal responsibilities.

Readiness Factor: Tolerance for Ambiguity

I can accept a lot of uncertainty around my job responsibilities.

| 1 | 2 | 3 | 4 | 5 |

I prefer that my job activities be spelled out so I know exactly what I'm supposed to be doing.

I can function easily when I don't know exactly what's expected of me. I enjoy the challenges uncertainty brings.

I understand that it might take a while for all the details of the team system to be worked out.

| 1 | 2 | 3 | 4 | 5 |

I'm not comfortable waiting. I need to know immediately what will happen to my job.

I believe planning and taking time up front to discuss all the details will result in a better system and perhaps a personal "win."

Readiness Factor: Skills Profile Match

Business Knowledge

I can identify my company's major customers and know what orders my work area needs to fill next month.

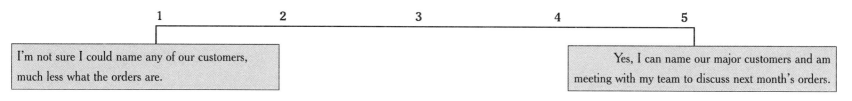

| 1 | 2 | 3 | 4 | 5 |

I'm not sure I could name any of our customers, much less what the orders are.

Yes, I can name our major customers and am meeting with my team to discuss next month's orders.

Interpersonal Skills

When I work with other people, I listen carefully to them, check my understanding, and maintain their self-esteem.

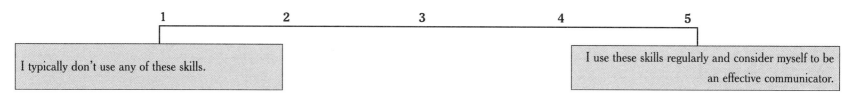

| 1 | 2 | 3 | 4 | 5 |

I typically don't use any of these skills.

I use these skills regularly and consider myself to be an effective communicator.

Team Skills

During meetings I'm able to help the group reach agreement by respecting everyone's differences, staying on track, and developing an action plan.

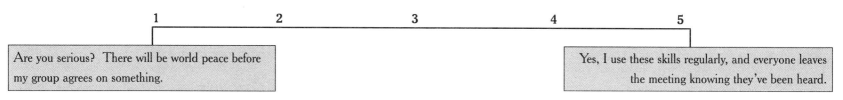

| 1 | 2 | 3 | 4 | 5 |

Are you serious? There will be world peace before my group agrees on something.

Yes, I use these skills regularly, and everyone leaves the meeting knowing they've been heard.

Problem Solving

When I'm faced with a problem, I examine its causes before coming up with a solution.

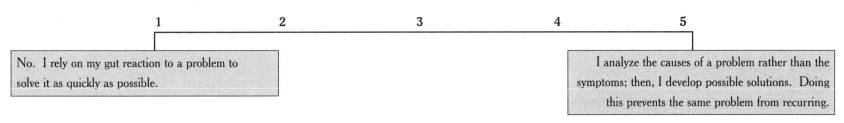

1	2	3	4	5

No. I rely on my gut reaction to a problem to solve it as quickly as possible.

I analyze the causes of a problem rather than the symptoms; then, I develop possible solutions. Doing this prevents the same problem from recurring.

Readiness Factor: Technical Skills

I understand my team's operation from start to finish and can competently perform my tasks as well as those of most other team members.

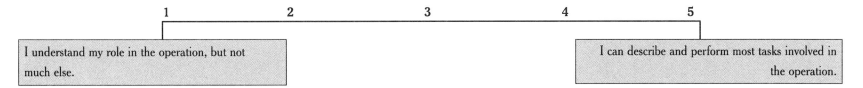

1	2	3	4	5

I understand my role in the operation, but not much else.

I can describe and perform most tasks involved in the operation.

Scoring Your Assessment: How You Stack Up

Step 1

To arrive at your final score, add the numbers of each response you circled.
Then refer to the following graph to see what your final score means.

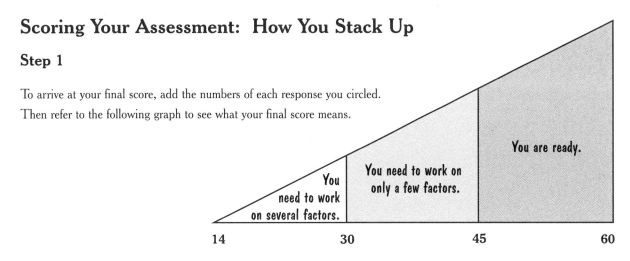

You are ready.

You need to work on
only a few factors.

You
need to work
on several factors.

14   30   45   60

Step 2

Now add the numbers you circled within each readiness factor and divide the total by the number of statements under that factor. For example, there are three statements for Increased Decision Making. If your numbers add up to 9, then your average readiness factor score for Increased Decision Making is 3 (9 ÷ 3 = 3). In the table on the next page, record your average score for each readiness factor in the "Average Score" column.

Refer to the following table to see if your readiness factor scores reveal a strength, an area for improvement, or whether you're treading water.

Readiness Factor Scores	
1 to 2.5	An area for improvement
2.6 to 3.5	Neither an area for improvement nor a strength, but something to keep an eye on
3.6 to 5.0	A clear strength to maintain

"One of the best things I did initially was to take advantage of feedback for improvement, even though my first instinct was to avoid it."

—Cement Manufacturing Operator

How to Improve Your Readiness Factor Scores

Ideally, all your readiness factor scores should be 3.6 to 5.0. But what if they're not? Use the table to the right to develop an action plan for improving your readiness factors. Then take this assessment again in three to six months. You'll see improvement if you follow the exercises in this guide.

To help steer you toward an effective plan, a suggested action item is included with each readiness factor.

Readiness Factors	Average Score	Examples of Ways to Maintain Strengths or Improve Weaknesses	Actions I Need to Take	By When
Increased Decision Making		Acquire additional technical information to help you become more capable and confident in your decision making.		
Working with Support Groups		Treat support groups more like internal customers; ask what their needs are.		
Willingness to Cross-Train		Start cross-training with an easy-to-learn skill and work up to more complex tasks.		
Tolerance for Ambiguity		This is a tough one. Try reviewing project plans to become familiar with what you can expect in upcoming months.		
Skills Profile Match		Attend team or interpersonal training and look for opportunities to apply your new skills the week after training.		
Technical Skills		Set aside time (at least one hour a week) with someone from your area to learn his or her job.		

Preteam Development Activity: Check Baggage Here

Introduction

Congratulations! You are on the brink of advancing to another stage of team evolution—the New Team Phase. You're making great strides, but before continuing to the next port of call on your development itinerary, you need to purge some of the "grudges" that are clogging your progress. For example, do you:

- Resent new employees or outsiders? (How could they know anything about how we work?)

- Still hold a grudge against another employee for something that happened in the fifth grade?

- Think they have all the answers, so why should they try to learn anything new?

If you are carrying this excess "baggage," don't worry. This short activity provides an easy way to lighten the load and smooth your transition to the New Team Phase.

Materials

Several Post-it™ notes for each person and one sheet of flip chart paper for the group.

Total Time Allotment

15 minutes for the group and 10 additional minutes per person.

Instructions

1. Ask everyone to read the activity introduction.

2. Ask each person to write his or her answers to the following two questions on a Post-it™ note (only one response per note). Allow about 15 minutes.

What baggage does your organization need to check?

Thought Starters:

- Status differences between classifications of workers; in one manufacturing company, supervisors (white hats) did not socialize with employees (blue hats).

- Treating employees differently depending on their level in the organization.

- Staking claim to the best pieces of equipment as your "territory" or taking the plum sales accounts for yourself.

-

-

-

-

What personal baggage do you need to check?

Thought Starters:

- Apathy because someone else always gets the prime opportunities.

- Feeling like I don't need to learn anything new.

- Thinking that I can cruise because the other team members will pick up the slack.

-

-

-

3. Ask for volunteers to read their answers aloud. After each answer is read, have the person put the Post-it™ note on the flip chart. Some people might not feel comfortable reading their answers aloud or having them posted on the flip chart. This is OK. To encourage team members and generate discussion, offer your own ideas for checking your baggage.

Optional

4. Save the flip chart and revisit the notes in six months to see if your team is sailing along unhindered or has stowed away some unwanted baggage.

Notes. . .

New Team Development Phase

You are now ready to launch into some unfamiliar seas, those of the newly formed teams. Over the next few months you and other team members will be sailing into new opportunities, and up to and around unfamiliar obstacles. Use the activities on the following pages to help steer through the narrows and straits of the first part of the New Team Phase.

Month 1

New Team Development: Team Survival Tips

Month 2

Changing Roles, Changing Focus

Month 3

Chartering Your Team: A Team Vaccination

Month 4

Focusing on Results

Month 5

Retooling Yourself for Teams

Month 6

Gaining Management Support

New Team Development Phase

What to Expect

Initial Excitement

In the Preteam Phase your organization was planning for teams. Now you're actually in teams, and the start-up can come as a relief after what seems an awful lot of planning and designing. The planning pays off now, as you have the foundation to do what teams are established to demonstrate in the first place: superior performance and flexibility.

Adjustments

We've talked about the adjustments in your daily routine resulting from the move to teams. Now is the time to put them into action. Don't delay. Start making changes that seem most "doable," such as spending 30 minutes a day cross-training within your team or tracking attendance for the team. Then learn more about the larger changes that

require more adjustments, such as working out of your area on a project or working with customers.

Don't expect that everyone will take on new tasks—such as leading meetings or organizing the team's weekly work—readily or easily. At first, some of your team members will pull their weight right away. Others will need more time to get into the new routine of taking more initiative or making more decisions. You'll be surprised what everyone can and will do—even people you might have thought were deadwood.

Possible Concerns

> I'm willing to give teams a go. But how are we going to meet output with all this extra work?

The time required for team skills training, cross-training, and team problem-solving meetings consumes about 10 percent of an average team member's time. However, if you work together, you can find ways to cover for each other's jobs. Here are some ideas:

- Take turns covering for each other, individually or for the entire team, where applicable.

- Ask supervisors to cover your jobs occasionally.

- Bring in qualified temps.

- Work moderate amounts of overtime during spaced training.

- Plan to attend training during downtimes in your operation or during periods of low customer demand.

What Will Teams Do to My Career?

Many people think the move to teams places a ceiling on their career. Not so. When you consider the options associated with teams, you'll find they enhance your ability to move around in your company and/or gain experience. This, in turn, can make you more valuable to the organization.

With teams, you get to:

- Cross-train, not only within your department, but in teams throughout your operation.

- Get involved with organizational design, team implementation, and/or enhancement; thereafter, you become a "teams guru."

- Take on new leadership tasks and roles.

- Work on projects to solve quality or customer-satisfaction issues.

- Work with people from different professional backgrounds, such as human resources, accounting, process engineering, laboratory, etc.

- Move into a project leader role.

- Move into a coach/team manager role.

- Become a technical expert on a team.

Teams invite plenty of opportunity. You simply need to think of the best way to take advantage of new opportunities that seem right for you.

New Team Development: Team Survival Tips

Notes. . .

Month 1

Ready or not, you're now about to "officially" launch your work in teams. One caution: It probably won't be as easy as you might have thought. You'll want to keep the Team Survival Tips in mind; they're still important, and they can be adapted as you progress to more advanced stages in your team's development. Here's how to apply the Team Survival Tips you learned in the Preteam Phase to your situation in the New Team Development Phase.

4. Full Speed Ahead

1. Getting Started

3. Getting on Course

2. Going in Circles

Team Survival Tips

1. **Become a quick-change artist.** Working in teams might require you to make slight or significant changes to your work procedures, who is responsible for leadership tasks, or who contacts support departments for needed resources. Keep an open mind and try to remain flexible. Make sure you understand how these changes affect your specific job; don't try to slide by doing things the old way. Use the space on the right to clarify what you'll be doing differently and what tasks/responsibilities you're still not sure about.

What changes can you expect to work procedures in your area?

Specifically, what are you responsible for doing differently?

1.

2.

3.

What are you still unclear about?

Are any of the steps you take in doing your work not adding value to your new team's configuration? Do they cause excess movement of materials or people, rework, or unnecessary review?

List three actions you can take to help your team eliminate non-value-adding steps.

1.

2.

3.

2. **Add value.** It's time to improve your personal cycle time. The entire group will be focusing more than ever on how each team member contributes to the overall goals. You can help your team add value by looking for better, more efficient ways of doing everything. Use the space on the right to organize your thoughts.

3. Take ownership for yourself and the company. At this point, you might not like everyone on your team. You might even consider some of your new teammates to be just plain deadwood. Like it or not, in a team environment you must take responsibility to work together as professionals. You have to use one another's strengths and work hard to improve one another's weaknesses. Take ownership for your team and yourself by recognizing the value that each member brings. Remember, your team is only as strong as its weakest link. What can you do to help improve the team overall? Use the space on the right to jump-start your thinking.

How can you show that you value other team members' contributions?

1.

2.

3.

List the unique skills that you bring to the team.

1.

2.

3.

4. **Become a lifelong learner.** You and your team can expect to make mistakes; what really matters is how you handle them. Instead of blaming others, you can help your team create a learning environment by "failing forward"— learning from mistakes. You and your team members will be a lot more likely (and willing) to work together if you can reduce the fear of failure. Establishing a learning environment in your team is a two-step process:

1) Fail forward by focusing on the problem, not blaming the person who made the mistake.

2) Document or review key learnings so that the mistake can be avoided in the future.

5. Manage your own morale. One of the easiest traps to fall into with new teams is to let your fears get the better of you. Moving forward in teams requires you to stick your neck out a bit. It's like you're putting yourself on the line for something you believe in (even if you're not sure that you do yet). At the same time, you might have fears or doubts about moving ahead. It can be very helpful at this point to identify your fears and determine what you can do to minimize them. Use the space on the right to help you.

What doubts or fears do you have about this stage of team development, and what can be done to dispel them?

Doubts/Fears	What can be done?
We're moving too fast—we're headed for chaos.	Refer to an implementation plan for key milestones.
1.	
2.	
3.	

• Your supervisor won't adapt perfectly to the move to teams. Most supervisors in the first few months of team implementations either move too slowly (they resist allowing team members to make decisions) or too quickly (the old "dump and run" syndrome when supervisors pass on too many tasks to team members who aren't ready for them).

• It might take 6–12 months before you see measurable, bottom-line results in your team.

• Your job will change as you move into teams, but it won't change overnight. Eventually, you'll probably learn more about cross-training and share leadership tasks.

Take a minute now to think about your expectations for the new team. Use the space below to help clarify your expectations.

6. Monitor your own expectations. Nobody likes a wet blanket—getting your hopes sky high only to have them dashed by disappointment. One of the biggest wet blankets in the New Team Development Phase is expecting too much, too soon. For example, at this point you or your team members might be expecting your supervisor to let you make all the decisions. The supervisor, on the other hand, probably hasn't had enough time to get comfortable with handing over some tasks to teams. To avoid disappointment for everyone, keep your expectations realistic. Here's what you can expect:

> What are your expectations at this point (be honest)?
>
>
>
>
> Which of these might be out of line and need to be reined in?

7. **Yell for what you need.** Don't stew over concerns, frustrations, or other issues. Bring them up with the team, even if you've mentioned them before. Work with the team to get the answers you need. And remember, your team members are not mind readers. Use the space on the right to help you organize your thoughts.

What issues/concerns do you have with the team?

How can you bring these up in a constructive way?

Changing Roles, Changing Focus

Notes...

Month 2

At the end of the Preteam Phase, we focused on redesigning your work flow and gauging your readiness to hoist anchor and move forward to work in a team-based environment. Both of these factors will play a big part in your success. The easiest way to sail ahead in your new team role is to:

1. Follow the redesign steps in Preteam Month 5 (eliminating non-value-adding tasks, removing bottlenecks, etc.).

2. Take action on any deficient-readiness factors.

By now you're probably spending a lot of time fighting frustration—working with inefficient and/or outdated

(traditional) processes. Eliminating even some of the bottlenecks can clear the decks for you to take on more important and interesting work or even cross-training.

How Your Role Is Changing

In the new team structure everyone's role—yours, your supervisor's, your manager's—changes dramatically. Your managers will be focusing more on bringing in new business and promoting your company's capabilities and less on the details of the operation. Your supervisors will take on responsibilities from managers, such as budgetary duties, vendor evaluations, and personnel issues. They'll also spend more time teaching employees how to run the operation. So, supervisors should be spending more time coaching you and your teammates how to handle the tasks you'll be responsible for later.

The diagram on the right shows how a telecommunications organization progressively changed the roles of its managers, supervisors, and team members in moving toward a team-based environment.

Managers

Expanded Responsibilities:

- Teach business awareness
- Create a five-year plan to increase customer and employee satisfaction
- Bring in new business
- Train customers

Keep:

- External bid preparation
- Budget review

Supervisors

Expanded Responsibilities:

- Vendor evaluation
- Monday update meetings
- New hires
- Customer satisfaction survey coordination

Keep:

- Bill payment
- Personnel issues
- Customer issues the team can't handle

Team Members

Expanded Responsibilities:

- Resolve problems with customers directly
- Schedule vacations
- Take action to improve team morale
- Train other team members
- Evaluate progress on team goals

Eliminate:

- Redundant work procedures
- Double counting on paperwork
- Dead time between jobs

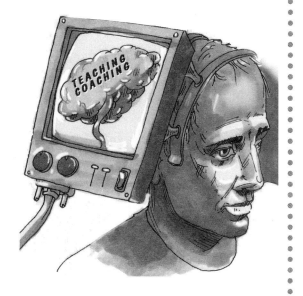

What's Different About Your Supervisor's Job?

Understanding what your supervisor will be doing differently can go a long way toward explaining what you'll need to focus on in your new role. In the typical New Team Development Phase, supervisors spend at least 50 percent of their time coaching employees to take on day-to-day tasks that either they or support professionals used to do. Supervisors spend a lot less time with administration because non-value-adding administrative tasks have been eliminated and because team members are taking on the remaining tasks. The pie charts below show the difference between the old and new roles of most supervisors.

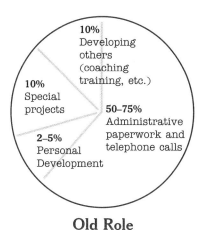

10%
Developing others (coaching training, etc.)

10%
Special projects

50–75%
Administrative paperwork and telephone calls

2–5%
Personal Development

Old Role

30%
Administrative paperwork and telephone calls

10–15%
Personal Development

50–60%
Developing others (coaching training, etc.)

15%
Special projects

New Role

How Your Role Changes

Successful team members readjust how they spend their time. To gauge how teams will affect the work you do, list all the value-adding tasks you perform on a typical day. Leave blank any of the headings below if they don't apply to you now.

How You Currently Spend Your Time

Tasks You Perform:

Administrative (paperwork, reports, phone calls, timecards, etc.):

1.
2.
3.
4.
5.

Operations (technical steps required to finalize your product or service):

1.
2.
3.
4.
5.
6.
7.
8.
9.
10.

Personal Development (classroom training, on-the-job training, etc.):

1.
2.
3.
4.
5.

Leadership Tasks (coordinating work or meetings for the team):

1.
2.
3.
4.
5.

Project Tasks (tasks required to complete safety, quality, or efficiency projects for your area or between areas):

1.
2.
3.
4.
5.

Team Member Job Profiles: Before Teams and After

Typically in the transition to teams, team members' jobs become more proactive, more interesting, and more valuable to the company. The profiles on the right are from an insurance company and will give you a feel for how your job might change when your teams are fully implemented.

Before

Before Teams	After Teams
Insurance sales position Focus of the role: • Offer services to current and prospective subscribers.	Sales linked to processing team Focus of the role: • Coordinate the sales process with the core processing team to ensure efficient customer service.
What people in this role should do more of: • Sell to the field customers.	What people in this role should do more of: • Learn what the computer system is capable of doing. • Touch base with communication star points about special offers and unusual benefits. • Explain the managed-care structure to the core team. • Use computer technology, such as e-mail, for communication to preferred reps and core team. • Consider the employees in the selling and delivery process as main customers/team members.
What people in this role should do less of: • Spend time in the field office instead of being out with field customers.	What people in this role should do less of: • Send in contracts late to internal customers. • Withhold information and expertise about customers.
Cross-training priority: • None.	Cross-training priority: • Operational understanding of setup and maintenance process. • Marketing analysis.

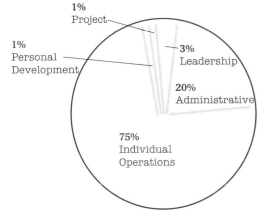

1%
Project

1%
Personal
Development

3%
Leadership

20%
Administrative

75%
Individual
Operations

Before Teams

With teams, the individual sales role on the left changed from reactive (administrative and "firefighting") to proactive (more collaboration to meet the customer's needs the first time). How will you be spending your time now that you'll be working as a team? Will your role become more interesting and proactive? Use the form on the next page to sketch out how you'll spend your time, on average, during the next six months.

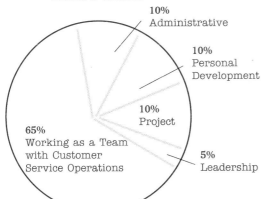

10%
Administrative

10%
Personal
Development

10%
Project

5%
Leadership

65%
Working as a Team
with Customer
Service Operations

After Teams

After

How You Will Spend Your Time in Teams

Tasks You Perform:

Administrative (paperwork, reports, phone calls, timecards, etc.):

1.
2.
3.
4.
5.

Operations (technical steps required to finalize your product or service):

1.
2.
3.
4.
5.
6.
7.
8.
9.
10.

Personal Development (classroom training, on-the-job training, etc.):

1.
2.
3.
4.
5.

Leadership Tasks (coordinating work or meetings for the team):

1.
2.
3.
4.
5.

Project Tasks (tasks required to complete safety, quality, or efficiency projects for your area or between areas):

1.
2.
3.
4.
5.

What You Can Do

You've already thought about eliminating non-value-adding tasks from your current role. You've thought about how you spend your time now and how you'll spend it in the future. What else can you do to move toward your new role? Ask your supervisor to help you and your team members complete the worksheets presented in this chapter.

Chartering Your Team: A Team Vaccination

Notes. . .

Month 3

Have you ever been on a group or a team where no one could seem to get the team operating on all cylinders? Even your team meetings—scheduled to get your team's motor started—flounder, causing the team to sputter or lose momentum in performance and discouraging team members. The best way to avoid team floundering is to "vaccinate" your team against these symptoms by developing and periodically revisiting a team charter. Even experienced teams can get a much-needed tune-up by reviewing their charter.

Is your team floundering? If you think it is, review the chart on the next page and see how a team charter can be a painless antidote.

How Can You Tell if a Team Is Floundering?	What Difference Can a Charter Make?
Meetings easily stray off course; team members don't follow up on action items.	Your charter lays out the ground rules for how meetings will function, including how agendas will be developed, who leads meetings, how agreement is reached on follow-up, etc.
Team members don't show up for or participate in meetings.	People tend to be more interested in attending meetings that accomplish many things in a short period of time. A charter sets the groundwork so that the team can focus on problem solving rather than continuously trying to get the team on track.
Team members are unwilling to do anything extra for the team, such as come in early or trade assignments.	The charter's ground rules define acceptable and unacceptable behavior. When a team establishes ground rules together, members are, in essence, making a promise or commitment to the team about what they personally agree to do. Because the team makes agreements publicly, there's more of a chance that team members will stick to their agreements.
Team members fail to keep track of production and/or quality performance.	One of the primary reasons team members fail to follow through on tracking performance is that they are unclear about their responsibilities. The responsibilities section of the charter spells out what needs to be done and who is responsible for doing it.
Responsibilities fall through the cracks because no one is specifically accountable for activities.	A charter forces the team to clearly define roles and responsibilities in a way that everyone understands who is responsible for what.

Creating Your Team Charter: Key Components

What to Do First

When developing your charter, consider what's worked well for teams you've been on. It could be a project team, a sports team, or a virtual team on which you were a member for a short time. What were the elements, or components, of the charter that contributed to the team's success? There are probably a few you can borrow for your team's charter. You'll also want to come up with several questions the team needs to answer, such as: Why does the team exist? How will the team resolve conflicts? and How do we accomplish our purpose? To keep your team from becoming swamped with unanswered questions, put together a list of resources to call for help.

A charter sets your team in motion and primes it for success. The tables on the next three pages provide a blueprint you can use to develop your team's charter.

Component Description	Questions the Team Needs to Answer	Where to Go for Help	When You Should Revisit This Component
Purpose Describes why a team exists; defines how a team will deliver its product or service.	• Why exactly does our team exist? • Who are our customers? • How is our team different or similar to other teams in this organization?	• Ask your supervisor for market share information and organizational changes that provide data for your purpose.	• When the team is considering taking on a new task. Refer to your purpose statement to make sure the new task links with your team's main objective. • When new members join the team.
Responsibilities Describe the responsibilities or outputs for which a team will be accountable.	• What do we have to do to accomplish the team's purpose? • What do we need to do to ensure that our product or service meets customer requirements?	• Ask your supervisor what tasks he or she is handing down to the team and when. • Develop a to-do list from sources of errors and bottlenecks in your process map (refer to Preteam Month 5).	• Any time members are confused about who is doing what. • Any time another team or department wants to know more about what your team does. • When the team feels unchallenged and wants to take on more challenging work.

Component Description	Questions the Team Needs to Answer	Where to Go for Help	When You Should Revisit This Component
Boundaries Clarify how much a team can do on its own and how much other people must be involved.	• What limits has management set for us? • What kinds of decisions can we make? • What kinds of decisions do we need to get approval for?	• Ask your supervisor what decisions are "out of bounds" for your team. • Seek agreement with other departments or shifts on who makes what decisions and when.	• When you want to try to improve relations between your team and another team or area. • When the team makes a mistake and wants to learn how to avoid the same mistake in the future. • When you get into "turf battles" with another department or a tug-of-war with your leader.
Ground Rules Define acceptable and unacceptable behavior within the team.	• How will our team make decisions? • How will we resolve conflicts? • What has been our worst team experience, and what should be done to prevent that from recurring?	• Ask someone from outside your team to observe your meetings and give you observations on the team's behavior. • Designate different team members to observe how the team adheres to the ground rules during meetings.	• When personal conflicts cause team meetings to stall out or disrupt work flow. • When conflicts that seemed to be resolved keep reigniting.

Component Description	Questions the Team Needs to Answer	Where to Go for Help	When You Should Revisit This Component
Meetings Describe the time, frequency, location, and rules of meetings.	• How often and for how long will we meet? • Where and when will we meet? • How often do we need to meet during the New Team Phase?	• Find out other team members' schedules to determine the best time for meetings. • Work with the team to determine the best way to minimize disruption to work schedules.	• When new members join the team. • During peak production periods. • If the team matures to the point of needing fewer meetings.

What to Do Next

Now it's your turn at the helm of the U.S.S. Charter. Fill in the spaces on the next page for each component of your team charter. You'll find it helpful to complete your team's purpose statement as a group. Then to save time, you might want to divide your team into pairs to work on each remaining component. This is not intended to be an all-encompassing document, so feel free to add components. When all the pairs have drafted their assigned component, review everything together as a team so everyone has input into the final charter.

Purpose:

Responsibilities:

Boundaries:

Ground Rules:

Meetings:

Other Components:

Now What?

Polish your work. Assign a subgroup of team members to edit and finalize the team's draft charter. It's important that the charter is clear enough so anyone outside the team can understand it.

Plan how you will use your charter with your team. Once your charter is in final form, decide as a group how to get the most out of it. Here are some ideas to consider:

- Discuss your charter with internal suppliers and customers to find out how your team can provide better service. This information further clarifies the charter's components, particularly boundaries and responsibilities.

- Use the charter to help orient new employees.

- Review your charter with your supervisor and managers to keep them up to speed on your team's initiatives.

- Schedule a charter review session in three months to check your team's progress on agreements you made.

Focusing on Results

Month 4

Your Business Plan

Your team, like any new business, probably will struggle to stay focused and accountable for its performance. One of the best approaches is to develop a team business plan, which targets goals for continuously improving your team's performance. Unlike the charter, which focuses on *how* your team will work together (purpose and ground rules), the team business plan focuses your team on *what* to do by *when*. It also identifies the people accountable for specific parts of the team's goals. When team members share accountability, the team is able to anticipate and solve problems before they create an undertow of issues that threaten to sink your team's progress.

Tired of that sinking feeling? Review the sample team business plan on the next page, then work through the business plan development steps with your team members. By the end of this chapter, you and your team will have your own business plan.

Sample Team Business Plan

Review Organizational Goals	Collect Baseline Performance Data	Develop Team Goals	Develop Action Plan	
Safety • No more than three recordables throughout the facility.	• Currently have no recordables. • New hires need safety training.	• Zero recordables in the next year. • Give new employees safety training during first week.	Pat: Don: Mary:	Conduct safety training quarterly. Restock safety equipment weekly. Plan next safety audit.
Quality • Reduce rejects by 10 percent.	• Current reject rate is 15 percent.	• Reduce rejects by 5 percent.	Pat: Don: Mary:	Learn to set specifications with greater accuracy. Implement two process improvements in his area that the team agrees to. Inspect product before it goes out.
Employee Involvement • Increase work teams' sense of ownership. • Make more use of employees' skills.	Star point functioning: • Each team member is learning one star point. • Increase team members' star point skills.	• All team members will rotate to at least one star point within the next six months.	Pat: Don: Mary:	Train Don as a backup on quality star point this summer. Document new safety procedures for the next star point to use. Meet with the facility accountant to discuss transition plan for the next star point.

Business Plan Development Steps

1. Review organizational goals.

First, collect your organization's goals (facility or division level) and your area's goals (department level) from your supervisor. These goals become the standards, or expectations, against which you can compare and adjust your team's performance. In turn, the goals your team develops will reflect its strengths and areas for improvement. This ensures that your team goals will be measurable, time bound, and doable.

Record this information in the first column of the blank worksheet at the end of this chapter.

2. Collect baseline performance data.

Data forms the baseline—a series of snapshots—for accurately measuring your team's progress. What type of performance data should your team track? Following are some examples of performance data that can benefit your team the most.

Examples of Performance Data

Measure Lead Time

Definition: The time it takes to transform an order or project idea to a completed product or service.

Current Department Goal: Cut lead time from three weeks to five days.

Actual Baseline Performance: Lead time reduced from three weeks to three days (*strength: actual performance exceeds the goal*).

Measure Rework

Definition: Work time devoted to repeating a task because it was not completed correctly (within customer requirements) the first time.

Current Department Goal: Increase first-pass yields (products or services completed accurately the first time) by 40 percent.

Actual Baseline Performance: First-pass yields increased by 30 percent (*needs improvement: actual performance does not meet the goal*).

To collect even better data, interview a representative sample of your internal and external customers about their needs. Their answers will give your team insight into whether they need to adjust goals or refocus on certain areas. Use the sample questions on the next page and add any that you think might be appropriate for your team's customers.

Sample Customer Interview Questions

- At what point (poor quality, poor customer service, late shipment) will you complain to your vendor?

- Over the last year, what specifically could our team have done more of to better meet your needs?

- How will your needs change in the next 12 months? What can we do to ensure that we still meet your needs?

-

-

In what areas has your team met or exceeded its goals, and where does it need improvement? Use the performance data you've collected to answer these questions in the spaces below. Then add this information to the second column of the blank worksheet at the end of this chapter.

Performance Areas in Which Goals Were Met or Exceeded (developing team goals for strengths will maintain strengths):

Performance Areas that Need Improvement (developing team goals here will improve performance):

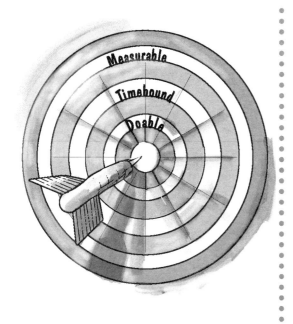

3. Develop team goals.

From this information determine what new goals or focus areas your team needs to add to its business plan and record them in the third column of the blank worksheet on the next page.

Use baseline data from customers or performance data collected over the last 12 months. Check to make sure your team goals are:

- *Measurable:* Allows you to check on how far your team has progressed toward achieving the goal. Measurements answer the questions *"How much?" "How many?"*

"What's the schedule?" and *"At what cost?"* Examples of measurements include the number of items produced, the number of incidents taking place, the accuracy or precision of actions, and revenue or expense accounts.

- *Time bound:* Lets you know when the goal needs to be achieved.

- *Doable:* Goals should have a balance between being too easy and too difficult to achieve. They should focus on actions over which team members have an appropriate degree of control.

4. Develop action plan.

Develop an action plan for each goal or focus and identify team members who can be responsible for each part of the plan.

Record this information in the fourth column of the blank worksheet below.

The individual actions in your team business plan will give you a clear sense of what you need to do to be an effective team member. The next chapter describes more of what effective team members are expected to do.

Review Organizational Goals	Collect Baseline Performance Data	Develop Team Goals	Develop Action Plan

Retooling Yourself for Teams

Notes. . .

New Competencies

There's no doubt about it: Jobs are changing radically. But are your skills keeping pace with the requirements needed to perform these jobs? If your answer to the question, "Can I be an effective performer in a high-performance, team-based job, role, or task?" is no, then you need to retool. Retooling can involve improving skills or adding new ones.

By improving your skills you'll be able to:

- Assume different roles in work assignments or on several teams (that is, be a project leader on one team and an as-needed subject expert on another team).

- Develop a framework for self-development as it relates to your own career planning.

- Adapt more quickly or effortlessly to changes in the organization and the job market.

You started new skill development in the Preteam Phase when you learned the importance of improving your work processes (Preteam Month 5) and completed the readiness assessment (Preteam Month 6). Now that you are in the New Team Phase, you might need to enhance your skills even further.

New Team Development Phase Competencies

There are three skill areas, or competencies, in which you'll need to improve in the New Team Phase:

- Problem Solving and Analysis

- Initiative

- Collaboration

Here's a brief description of each.

Problem Solving and Analysis: Finding relevant information and identifying key issues and relationships from a database; comparing data from different sources to identify trends and cause-and-effect relationships.

Key Behaviors

- **Identify issues and problems.** Recognize major issues, identify key facts and trends, and separate relevant from irrelevant data.

- **Seek information.** Identify information gaps, obtain information by clearly describing what you need to know and knowing where to get the it, and follow up clearly and specifically to confirm information.

- **See relationships.** Organize information and data to identify and explain trends, problems, and their causes; compare, contrast, and combine information; recognize trends among seemingly unrelated problems or events.

To demonstrate effective problem-solving and analysis skills, you need to:

- Analyze relationships among several parts of a problem or a situation.

- Systematically break down a complex task into manageable parts.

- Recognize several likely causes of problems and several consequences of possible solutions.

- Anticipate barriers and develop contingency plans.

> The next opportunity you'll have to demonstrate your problem-solving and analysis skills is:

To fine-tune your performance in this competency:

- Attend quality-improvement training, which includes instruction on assessing the situation, gathering data, and using problem-solving tools (pareto diagrams, fishbone diagrams, etc.). Quality-improvement training will give you a format to guide you through finding the root cause of any problem.

- Use the process mapping tools you learned in Preteam Month 5 to gather data about your process. This data can pinpoint trends and relationships of problems such as cycle time, backlog, output, and quality.

Now add your own ideas for improving your performance in this competency.

-

-

-

Initiative: Asserting one's influence over events to achieve goals; self-starting rather than accepting passively; taking action to achieve goals beyond what is required; being proactive.

Key Behaviors

- **Seek understanding.** Ask questions/Seek information to understand work processes and organizational issues; identify resources and information that might be of assistance in future initiatives undertaken.

- **Identify opportunities.** Seek and recognize opportunities for action both within and outside present work assignments.

- **Assume responsibility.** Take action on identified opportunities; respond to problems encountered by taking action to ensure they are resolved.

- **Ensure success.** Choose extra assignments/task that have some chance of success; takes appropriate actions to successfully complete initiatives undertaken (e.g., involve stakeholders).

To demonstrate effective initiative, you need to:

- Frequently seek to better understand work processes and organizational issues in order to identify opportunities for improvement.

- Take action independently in response to problems/opportunities within your own job area and usually persist in efforts until success is achieved.

- Take action beyond what is required in the job, but occasionally fail to take necessary action to ensure success.

The next opportunity you'll have to demonstrate your initiative is:

To fine-tune your performance in this competency:

- Use bottleneck analysis to identify problems you can act on or help others solve.

- Think about what your team needs to do next.

Now add your own ideas for improving your performance in this competency.

-
-
-

Collaboration: Working effectively and cooperatively with others; building relationships that facilitate the achievement of work goals.

Key Behaviors

- **Subordinate personal goals.** Place higher priority on team or organization goals rather than own goals.

- **Volunteer assistance.** Offer assistance to help others achieve mutual goals.

- **Use Key Principles.** Establish good interpersonal relationships by helping people feel valued, appreciated, and included in discussions (maintain or enhance self-esteem, empathize, involve, disclose, support).

To demonstrate effective collaboration, you need to:

- Work with men and women from different ethnic or cultural backgrounds; value and draw upon diversity among individuals.

- Perform tasks that require cooperating with others.

- Assist a coworker by temporarily filling in as needed.

- Seek, share, and accept constructive suggestions and assistance.

- Communicate changes or problems to peers or other team members.

- Encourage others.

- Model team values.

- Work with others to achieve team goals; place team goals ahead of personal needs.

- Recognize the efforts of others and praise and reinforce good performance.

- Develop teamwork and cooperation by involving others, encouraging their contributions, and communicating regularly with them.

- Show empathy when others encounter difficult situations.

- Facilitate cooperation within and among teams.

- Assist team members.

The next opportunity you'll have to demonstrate your collaboration is:

To fine-tune your performance in this competency:

- Attend skills training in areas such as reaching consensus, team effectiveness, resolving conflict, communicating with others, and building trust.

- Ask someone to give you honest feedback on how collaborative you've been (within the past six months).

- Share information or expertise you have with someone on your team who needs help solving a problem or is cross-training.

Now add your own ideas for improving your performance in this competency.

-

-

-

Gaining Management Support

Notes. . .

Bulletin: Not all struggles team members have are with other team members. In fact, their greatest challenge might be getting the necessary support from their supervisors or managers. As you learn what it takes to be an effective team member, your boss probably is learning the ropes of effective team leadership. Don't assume, though, that your boss has all the coaching skills under his or her belt. Occasionally, you might need to prompt or coach your boss to get the support you and your team need.

At this point most teams are looking for help in these areas:

- Getting time to cross-train.

- Gaining computer access.

- Solving conflicts between departments.

- Gaining business knowledge.

- Networking with others in the organization to solve a problem.

- Getting approval for equipment purchases.

Don't panic about your potential coaching duties—there is a dual benefit. While your team will receive the support it needs, your boss will be on his or her way to becoming a successful high-involvement leader.

Why No Management Support?

While it might be easy to say, "Management just doesn't care," it's certainly not practical to paint with such a broad brush. Think of the areas in which you need management support. The list on the next page might help you spot the areas if you're unable to cite specifics. Check any of these symptoms that apply to your situation.

☐ **Totally Clueless Syndrome:** Some managers might not fully understand all the work your team has accomplished or your current projects. Therefore, they might not always offer the help you were expecting or hoping for.

☐ **Hard-Core Autocracy:** Does your boss act like Captain Hook? Bosses who seem unwilling to allow team members to make significant decisions are practicing hard-core autocracy.

☐ **Inconsistent "Backslidingitis":** This is a symptom of bosses who believe they are effective team leaders, but tend to backslide into a traditional management style. Backsliders might phase in and out of a support role, depending on how critical the situation or decision is.

.Now think of your team. What are its biggest management support issues? Check any of the following that apply and add any that aren't listed.

☐ Need more time for team training or cross-training.

☐ Encouragement to make administrative/operational decisions.

☐ Reinforcement on the team's decisions.

☐ A clearer path for directly communicating with suppliers and customers.

☐ A clearer path for directly communicating with internal department heads.

☐

☐

☐

What Can You Do to Improve Management Support?

Does it seem like you're stranded on a sailboat on a still day when it comes to seeking support from your boss? Don't send out an SOS yet. The following suggestions should help get you the necessary support. Check the suggestions on this page that might work for your team and add any ideas you have on the next page.

☐ Schedule regular progress meetings with your boss to discuss expectations.

☐ Provide status reports on how your team is progressing with its business plan.

☐ Include time during team meetings for feedback from your boss on the team's performance.

☐ Demonstrate your team's decision-making skills by collecting the necessary data and updating your boss throughout the decision-making process.

☐ Make a realistic list of support your team needs to carry out its business plan (for example, resources, time, materials, meetings with other departments) and discuss it with your boss.

☐ Show your boss how the team's activities and accomplishments link to specific business goals that are important to him or her.

☐ Offer suggestions along with requests for resources. For example, if you need several team members to attend a daylong technical training class, suggest what can be done to maintain productivity in their absence.

☐ Ask members from other teams or departments for their ideas on gaining management support.

Your Ideas

☐

☐

☐

☐

☐

Your Team's Management Support Plan

Now it's time to put your ideas to work. One of the most effective ways to do this is to put together a plan that outlines which team members will do what by when to gain management support. Use the sample in the table on the next page as a stepping-stone to your team's plan, which you can complete in the blank table. You may include as many activities as you feel are necessary.

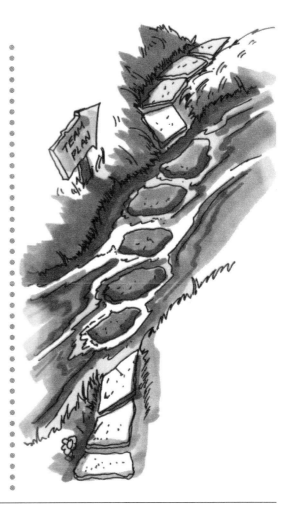

Sample Management Support Plan

Issue	Gaining Support Activity	Who Is Responsible	By When
The team needs more time for cross-training during regular work hours.	Present a plan to management that shows how we can maintain production and achieve our cross-training goals by having certain team members cover high-volume areas. Our goal is to gain Terri's commitment to allowing time to cross-train.	Bob, Sherri, and Kate will develop the training coverage plan and have it typed. The plan must link cross-training to our company's objectives of first-time accuracy and quality.	The team will present and discuss the plan with Terri, our supervisor, at our next staff meeting in two weeks.

Your Team's Management Support Plan

Issue	Gaining Support Activity	Who Is Responsible	By When

New Team Development Activity: "Used to Be," "As Is," and "Will Be"

Introduction

By now your team should really be starting to gel. Sure, there still might be some days when you can't even shove off without getting off course, but for the most part, your team is steaming right along. At this point you'll want to determine why the team performs well at some points and not so well at others. One of the best ways to do this is to get the whole team's perspective on where you *have been* as a team, where you *are now*, and where you *would like to go* next. Expect differing perceptions of how the team is functioning. Drawing out the history of your team can reveal underlying problems and bring issues—good and bad—out in the open.

Materials

One sheet of flip chart paper and a marker for each team member.

Total Time Allotment

20 minutes as a team and 10 additional minutes per team member to discuss his or her view.

Instructions

1. Explain that this is a chance for all team members to "show their cards." That is, each member can sketch how he or she feels the team is progressing or functioning.

2. Ask each team member to draw a picture describing how he or she sees the team's progress—from where it used to be, to where it currently is, to where it will be. Each team member will draw three pictures. Share the example on the next page.

One Team Member's Drawing:

Our Team Used to Be: Frustrated
baseball players are sitting in the dugout.

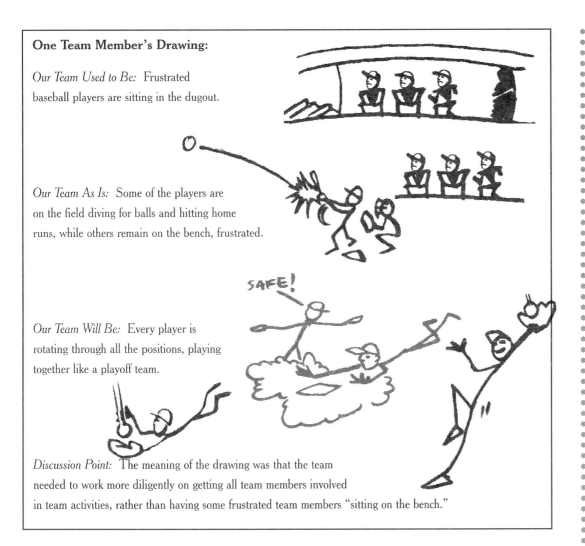

Our Team As Is: Some of the players are
on the field diving for balls and hitting home
runs, while others remain on the bench, frustrated.

Our Team Will Be: Every player is
rotating through all the positions, playing
together like a playoff team.

Discussion Point: The meaning of the drawing was that the team
needed to work more diligently on getting all team members involved
in team activities, rather than having some frustrated team members "sitting on the bench."

3. Distribute the flip chart paper and markers to all team members and allow 20 minutes for the team to draw all three pictures.

Our Team Used to Be:

Our Team As Is:

Our Team Will Be:

4. At the end of 20 minutes, ask team members to post their drawings. Then:

    • Ask one team member to document issues on a flip chart. The chart should be set up as follows:

What Works Well for Our Team	What Could Be Improved
•	•
•	•
•	•

    • Ask each team member to discuss the meaning of his or her drawings. Allow each person 5 to 10 minutes for discussion.

5. Ask the team which one or two items from the issues chart they want to develop action items for. Make sure you assign who will do what by when.

Notes. . .

New Team Maintenance Phase

Congratulations! By now you and your team should be sailing on an even keel. During the next seven months your team will not only discover the secrets of gaining momentum, you'll also chart new territory. Use the activities on the following pages to guide you through the New Team Maintenance Phase.

Month 7

New Team Maintenance:
Team Survival Tips

Month 8

Getting on Course: Tackling New Tasks
and Mastering Team Meetings

Month 9

Working Smarter with Suppliers
and Customers

Month 10

Gathering Speed: Negotiating
with Your Customers

Month 11

Making Decisions and Handling
Work Habits Issues as a Team

Month 12

Picking Up Speed: Managing Your Time

Month 13

Taking Initiative as a Team

New Team Maintenance Phase

What to Expect

Your team has experienced stormy swells, blustery winds, and maybe even a typhoon or two as you've struggled to maintain an even keel. That's all behind you—the team should be headed for smoother sailing! After the conflict and confusion of the New Team Development Phase, you and the team have probably sorted out roles and responsibilities and now can spend more time focusing on getting things done. You'll feel more productive and less frustrated as the team really buckles down over the next few months. You'll finally be able to bask in the satisfaction of some real team accomplishments.

4. Full Speed Ahead

1. Getting Started

3. Getting on Course

2. Going in Circles

Possible Concerns

> I can't believe it! Just when we got our old leader trained, she gets promoted. Now we're going to have to start all over again with somebody new. Isn't there anything we can do to make this any easier?

You bet! You can jump-start the process with the new leader by using what many teams call an "inclusion process." It's designed to speed up the adjustment period by facilitating an open discussion right from the start. (This process also works quite well when a team is bringing in new members.)

Before the first meeting with your new leader:

- Ask a neutral facilitator to help you. (This can be someone from human resources, another team, or even your old leader.)

- Have the facilitator collect questions and concerns from team members (for example, "Will the new leader be comfortable with the degree to which we manage ourselves?").

- Have the facilitator collect questions and concerns from the new leader (for example, "I've heard that this team is pretty rowdy and irreverent—is that true?").

- If your team uses a personal style inventory, have the facilitator collect a style profile from the new leader and display it on a chart with current team members' styles.

At the first meeting:

- Welcome the new leader and ask everyone to introduce themselves. You might suggest that team members share a humorous story of how it felt the first day they joined the team.

- Review the team's charter, operating guidelines, Empowerment Schedule, and training plan.

- Review the team's style profile and discuss how the new leader's style fits in; identify the leader's strengths that will benefit the team.

- Have the facilitator ask the questions the team has prepared for the new leader (and make sure that all the questions get adequate discussion).

- Have the facilitator ask the questions the new leader has prepared for the team.

- Ask the facilitator to summarize any hopes, concerns, and expectations, and then agree on how the team and the new leader will follow up to ensure that expectations on both sides are being met.

There are two keys to making this new relationship succeed:

- Being open about expectations.

- Arranging for frequent, two-way feedback in the early going.

You might be reluctant to approach the new leader with concerns; if so, it might help to ask the facilitator to return for at least one meeting one to three months after the new leader starts.

New Team Maintenance: Team Survival Tips

Notes. . .

Month 7

By now the Team Survival Tips we discussed in the Preteam and New Team Development Phases should have paid some dividends for you. Now that you are in teams, there might be heavy pressure for you to continue to perform. How do you keep those results coming? The Team Survival Tips on the following pages can help you as the team moves forward.

Team Survival Tips

1. **Become a quick-change artist.** Been there, done that, you say? Be careful not to rest on your laurels just yet. Often after organizations implement teams, a change in the structure or workload will come at you from nowhere. How does your team adapt to new team members who might come on board as the result of a merger? What if the team is working on a new application or product? You can tell a team is effective if the members use

what they've learned in the Preteam Phase. That is, your team should be able to respond to significant changes more quickly now than when you were a new team. How do you do that? The following checklist can help.

Quick-Change Artist Checklist

☐ Use your team's documentation and charter to recharter yourself with new members. Quickly modify the charter to include new responsibilities, ground rules, and goals.

☐ Review the team's business plan with new members or new suppliers. A tangible plan is easier for a new person to grasp than starting from scratch with a blank piece of paper.

☐ Use the team's knowledge to anticipate tough situations and brainstorm approaches to tackle problems that are likely to occur given the changes coming your way.

☐ Think of ways your team can apply training skills you've gained to new situations. For example, if your company is going through a merger and your team will be adding new members, you might use the reaching agreement tools you learned early on to prioritize high-impact and low-effort steps and acclimate new team members quickly.

☐ If your team is facing new tasks, consider dividing and conquering. In the past you might have used subgroups of team members to tackle many tasks. As long as groups within your team understand their task(s) and then make sure to share information as they regroup with the larger team, dividing into subgroups can be an effective way to get a lot done.

☐ What does your team need to do?

2. **Add value.** New teams need to focus on going beyond the "low-hanging fruit" (a.k.a. fat rabbits). By that we mean your team already might have solved some of the most obvious quality or productivity bottlenecks. Now is the time to develop a plan for tackling more complex, defect-related, or work-coordination problems. Working on these problems will add boatloads of value. Here's one way to get started:

- Think of situations that occur among teams, departments, or work groups that might be "ripe" work-coordination problems. Get your team together with others who are affected by these problems and develop an improvement plan.

Major work problems between teams are (jot down some of those you've encountered):

The first steps to take with a team from another area would be:

1) Use your process map to isolate problems between work areas that cause major cost inefficiencies. Review the problems with your supervisor and get his or her support.

2) Review the process map with other affected teams.

3) Develop a purpose statement that your joint teams will use to develop an action plan.

3. **Take ownership for yourself and the company.** By now you should be more comfortable with working in teams. Now is the time to take ownership—not only of your team's process and more responsibilities, but of some of the big picture. Make sure you don't lose sight of how your team fits in with the rest of the company. Some teams bond together so tightly (we call it "overbonding"), they alienate other teams.

Symptoms of Overbonding

You might have a problem with overbonding if:

- You hear other people refer to your team as a clique.

- Your team has been known to steal resources (equipment, materials, etc.) from other teams.

- It's been months since you've acted on an idea from outside the team.

- Lately, your team meetings resemble pro football touchdown celebrations.

- You disregard or downplay suggestions from anyone outside your team.

4. **Become a lifelong learner.** So far, this tip has meant learning more about teams and developing a learning organization within your team. What can the team focus on now that you're established? Set your sights beyond the team's boundaries. Here are some ideas people on your team can apply to advance their learning:

- Learn more about how suppliers develop materials used in your process.

- Visit some customers to learn more about how they use your products or services.

- Get information about developments in government regulations or laws relative to your products or services.

- Find out how your company's stocks are performing.

- Enroll a team member in a college course pertaining to a skill in your team's cross-training plan.

- Contact international employees in your company via e-mail or the Internet to learn how they solve similar problems overseas.

5. **Manage your own morale.** You can expect to feel more competent and in control at this stage of the team's development. Team results should be improving by now, so you also can enjoy the recognition that comes with doing a good job. Find ways to keep the goal of making progress on everyone's mind; this will help your team remain fresh and prevent "team burnout" down the road. Here are some examples:

- At every team meeting make sure someone mentions the good work the team has done.

- Continually remind yourself how far your team has come. One way to do this is to display photographs that depict your progress.

- Send team members a surprise message or e-mail commending their hard work.

6. **Monitor your own expectations.** Because some teams develop more quickly than others, not everyone will be up to speed yet. If it hasn't happened yet for your team, don't lose heart—it will.

Some team members frustrate themselves and their teammates by expecting too much too soon. Learn to balance high expectations with realistic results. Use the guide on this page to gauge the level of your expectations.

Expectations Normal for Teams in the New Team Maintenance Phase	Expectations More Characteristic of Teams in the Mature Team Phase
• Moderately productive team meetings • Still some interpersonal conflicts • Improving—but not stellar—performance results • Some lingering confusion about roles and responsibilities, but less than before	• Productive—sometimes even enjoyable—team meetings • Most conflicts within the team have been—or are being—resolved • Meeting or exceeding performance goals • Little or no confusion about roles and responsibilities

If you have additional concerns or expectations about the team's workings that are not reflected above, note them here and discuss them with the team:

Notes. . .

7. **Yell for what you need.** Now that you're starting to get the hang of this, it'll be increasingly apparent to you and the team what additional resources you need to function even better. In the last phase you were in the position of "we don't know what we don't know." Now at least you know what you don't know!

The key, of course, is to **ask for it**! Take time now to consider what you and the team could use to become even more effective. Jot down some notes on the grid on the next page and discuss your ideas with the team. Use the example as a guide.

What three things would you want to help the team become more effective?	In reality, who would you need to speak to in your organization to make this happen?	How would you present the team's case? What would compel this person to help you?
Example: We need another computer terminal.	Ed, our point of contact in Information Technology.	We could do 25 percent of the work that we send to IT. This would save IT 120 hours of work a year and enable our team to produce its weekend results and production schedule much more quickly.

Getting on Course: Tackling New Tasks and Mastering Team Meetings

Notes. . .

Month 8

Are all team members still speaking to each other? Good! Then you're probably over the hump by now. You've gotten the hang of working with each other and have weathered much of the internal strife that characterizes the Going in Circles phase. Without having to expend so much energy on resolving team conflicts, the team should be ready to speed up its development. This is a good time to

look at taking on some new responsibilities and boosting your team meetings to the next level of effectiveness.

Continuing to Evolve

What?! You mean we've got to change again? I've barely had time to adjust to the first round of changes!

Sorry—it's not your grandfather's workplace anymore. The idea of doing the same job for 20 or 30 years has gone the way of the slide rule, the manual typewriter, and the black-and-white television. They might be in only one or two stores, but no one's buying them. And all we can say is, "Thank goodness!" Who wants to be doing the same boring job over and over again, anyway?

How do you know if you and the team are ready to tackle some new tasks? Use the following checklist to find out.

You

☐ You're competent in at least 70 percent of the team's current tasks.

☐ The last time you learned something new was more than three months ago.

☐ You have a list of "to do" items from the team and your supervisor that you never get to.

☐ Your leader has been asked to take on more responsibilities that will require him or her to be off-site even more than he or she is now.

☐ You don't feel as challenged as you used to.

☐ You're not as busy as you were three months ago.

☐ There are several things other people are doing that you'd like to learn.

The Team

☐ The team hasn't made a serious mistake in more than three months.

☐ The majority of team members are competent in their roles.

☐ We've started working more and more with teams outside our area.

☐ We've solved about 60 percent of the "low-hanging fruit" problems.

☐ Our team is capable of doing more.

☐ Most team members have completed their basic training.

☐ We don't rely on the leader as much as we used to.

Interpreting the Checklist

If you've checked three or more items, you and/or your team are ready to take on more responsibility.

If you're ready and the team isn't: You might want to volunteer for special assignments at team meetings or meet with the leader to discuss some tasks he or she is performing now that you might be able to take on.

If the team is ready and you aren't: You might want to review the cross-training plan during a team meeting. You can concentrate on perfecting your skills while performing some of the team's current tasks; meanwhile, other members can add new tasks to the plan and start developing the skills to handle them.

Where do these new responsibilities come from?

Use the table on the right to help plan what new responsibilities you might want to consider. After reading the examples, use the space provided to write in some specific new responsibilities for you and your team.

Sources of new things to do	Examples	Specific ideas for you and the team
• Things your leader is doing now that you find interesting or challenging, or that would enable you to better understand the team's operation.	• Track the team's performance against budget.	
• Things now being done by support groups (but which cause problems for your team).	• Attend the weekly production meeting.	
• The next group of items on your organization's Empowerment Schedule.	• Take over one of purchasing's responsibilities, such as reordering nonroutine supplies.	
	• Learn how to do your own vacation scheduling.	

> ## If we're doing all this new stuff, what's the leader getting paid for, anyway?

This is a common concern of many team members, particularly as the leader moves farther away from the team's daily work. Your leader should be taking on more responsibility too: things that had been done by higher-level leaders. However, if you feel this way about the leader, don't let resentment or suspicion fester. Here are some suggestions for clearing the air with your leader:

- At the next team meeting ask your leader to describe how his or her job is changing.

- Switch places with your leader for a day. (This will give both of you a better appreciation for each other's work.)

- Develop a chart with moveable tasks (you can use self-sticking note pads) to show what happens as: the leader assumes new responsibilities, some of the leader's responsibilities transfer to the team, and some tasks simply become obsolete.

As you've read about how and when to begin taking on new responsibilities, you've probably gotten the idea (bingo!) that team meetings are an important forum and vehicle for working out these kinds of issues. That is, provided your team is ready to hold productive meetings.

The Evolving Nature of Team Meetings

Remember those awkward, nothing-ever-gets-done, early team meetings? They're not a joyous occasion for most teams. Fortunately, most teams get better at conducting meetings—at least to the point where they're not embarrassing or painful anymore. And (we know this is hard to believe) if you work at them, meetings actually can be one of the most satisfying and important activities your team undertakes (no, we're not joking!).

One reason most teams have not achieved this heavenly state by this point in their development is because they spend entirely too much time just reporting information. You know what we mean: One team member drones on for 15 minutes about the safety report, followed by another team member recapping the team budget for 10 minutes. No wonder nobody wants to attend these bore-a-thons!

One of the hallmarks of more mature teams is that they spend a larger chunk of their meeting time actually solving problems and making decisions. In fact, by now at least half of the time spent in your team meetings should be devoted to deciding as opposed to merely discussing. Use the table on the right to evaluate your team's performance.

Type of Team Action	Examples	Expected Performance	Your Team
Reporting Information	"Let me fill you in on the management meeting . . ." "I'll review our service scores for the last quarter . . ." "Let's review the customer requirements . . ."	No more than 50 percent of the time in your team meetings should be spent on reporting information.	
Solving Problems/ Making Decisions	"So what are we going to do differently?" "What are we agreeing to do to fix that?" "From now on, we're going to . . ."	At least 50 percent of your time should be spent making decisions or solving problems.	

Moving on to higher-level issues in team meetings is no guarantee that your team won't have its share of frustration to vent. In fact, the most likely place for frustration to rear its ugly head is in a team meeting. Don't get discouraged—there are ways to keep your cool in even the most maddening meeting situations. The Team Member Sanity Check on the next few pages will help.

Team Member Sanity Check

Do you sometimes wonder if this team business is driving you crazy? Are you occasionally overwhelmed by the impulse to lock the rest of your teammates in a padded cell? Do you harbor fleeting homicidal impulses (particularly during full-team meetings)?

Actually, these feelings are perfectly normal (provided, of course, that you don't act them out). But the goal here is to reduce frustration and help you develop a sense of control over the team's work.

Consider the following common causes of team members "losing it." See if any apply to your team (check all that do); then, follow the suggestions listed to address the issue(s) you checked before it gets out of hand.

Insanity Trigger #1:

☐ ***Some members aren't pulling their weight.***

This is probably the biggest cause of frustration in most teams. Ironically, not all team members agree on who the sluggards are. People are often surprised when they're lumped into this group.

How to remain sane:

- Use your next team meeting as a forum to discuss a process for distributing the workload fairly. (Some teams keep an alphabetical list of team members and automatically give the next assignment to next person on the list.)

- Determine whether this is really a problem of not valuing someone else's differences. (Perhaps you do more work because you feel no one else can do it as well as you.)

- If there is only one team member at the root of this problem, speak to him or her privately (using the steps described in New Team Month 5).

Insanity Trigger #2:

☐ *Nobody on the team keeps their commitments.*

It's not uncommon for teams at this stage to be adept at coming up with plans—but relatively poor at executing them. However common this might be, failing to keep commitments can be fatal to a team. Make sure to take action now!

How to remain sane:

- Give people the benefit of the doubt: Assume they have forgotten what they agreed to do. Many teams publish a list of commitments after each meeting. As an alternative, keep a "Commitment Board" in your team area with names and dates to help keep everybody honest.

- Sometimes members don't keep commitments because they feel pressured into agreeing to unreasonable deadlines. This can happen for a variety of reasons: leadership pressure, a team norm of trying to one-up the next person, and so on. Often, simply acknowledging the problem in a team meeting and agreeing to new, more effective norms will be enough.

- On the other hand, failure to honor commitments sometimes is a symptom of a deeper problem: someone's lack of commitment to or dissatisfaction with the team. In these cases you might need an experienced facilitator who can help diagnose the problem and recommend specific corrective action.

Insanity Trigger #3:	If Someone Is . . .	You Can . . .
☐ ***These meetings are killers!***	Floundering	• Use an agenda. • Check the process. • Encourage others to help get the meeting on track.
Team meetings are often described in terms that sound more appropriate for instruments of medieval torture.	Wandering	• Prepare a detailed agenda and stick to it. • Set ground rules for personal conversations. • Suggest a return to the agenda item.
How to remain sane:	Dominating	• Set ground rules for sharing meeting time. • Encourage the participation of others who have said little. • Politely interrupt the dominating person and suggest that you move on.
To prevent this kind of pain, attend meeting leadership and participation training. Trust us—effective meeting participation is not a talent that comes naturally to most people. If you've already been through training but are still having problems, consider the following list	Withdrawing	• Give everyone sufficient information and materials beforehand. • Encourage the person to contribute. • Ask for the person's help.
of problems and remedies.	Feuding	• Meet the feudists beforehand to stress the impact of their behavior on the meeting. • Encourage the feudists to listen and respond with empathy. • Interrupt the arguing, if necessary, and refocus on the meeting goal.

Working Smarter with Suppliers and Customers

Notes. . .

Finally! The months you've invested in your team's development are paying off as you and the team begin to hit a steady stride. You should even notice some signs of synergy, where the sum of your combined efforts is actually greater than the sum of your individual parts. Now that your internal machinery is beginning to hum, it's time to focus on issues external to the team. This is a good month to start improving your relationships with suppliers and customers.

Getting Better Connected with Your Internal Suppliers

The conflict between the Hatfields and McCoys has nothing on the average interdepartmental rivalry. These feuds often have long and difficult-to-trace histories, but are accepted as a matter of fact by the parties in the respective camps. Much of the friction often stems from misunderstandings about needs and requirements. ("We've never gotten along with those clowns. They just don't understand what we need to do our jobs.") Unfortunately, these rivalries also have a way of making work lives miserable and getting in the way of results.

You can make your team's work easier if you improve your relationships with your internal partners. Start by determining who they are. In the space below list all the internal teams or departments that supply your team with information, products, or services.

Now that you've listed your internal partners, think about how often you or your team has complained, "If only (insert one of the partners) would (insert solution to complaint), our jobs would be a lot easier."

The irony is that these other groups probably are saying similar things about your team!

With all these negative feelings bubbling beneath the surface, it makes sense that improving the working relationship would benefit everyone. The questions on the next two pages will guide your attempt to do this. Work through each question for each of your internal suppliers (you can make photocopies of the blank form). When you don't have complete or up-to-date information, use this time to get it from your internal partners.

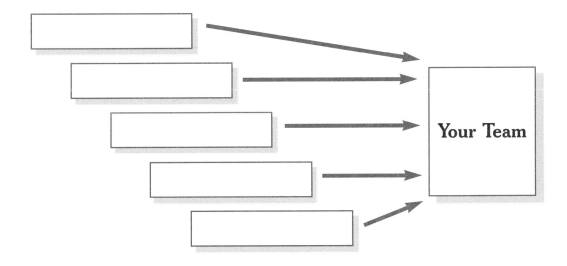

Internal Supplier Checklist

Supplier: _____

☐ What are this supplier's requirements? (What do they need from your team to do their job?)

_____

_____

_____

_____

How would you rate your team's performance meeting these requirements?

☐ Less than acceptable   ☐ Acceptable   ☐ More than acceptable

How would your supplier rate your team's performance meeting these requirements?

☐ Less than acceptable   ☐ Acceptable   ☐ More than acceptable

What does this supplier want your team to:

☐ do more of? _____

_____

☐ do less of? _____

_____

☐ continue doing? _____

_____

☐ What requirements does your team have for this supplier? (What does your team need from the supplier to do their job?)

_____

_____

_____

_____

How would you rate the supplier's performance meeting these requirements?

☐ Less than acceptable ☐ Acceptable ☐ More than acceptable

What does the team want this supplier to:

☐ do more of? _____

_____

☐ do less of? _____

_____

☐ continue doing? _____

_____

You and your teammates can forge stronger relationships with your internal suppliers by following two simple steps:

1. **Ask about the supplier's requirements** and how your team is meeting them. Often this feedback alone improves the relationship by 50 percent because it demonstrates your interest and concern. Not only that, but most of the time you and the team will learn something in the process.

2. **Make a commitment to change** at least one "do more of" and one "do less of" item that you listed. And be sure to follow through on your promise. After you've made these improvements, schedule a meeting to discuss your team's requirements. Here's a sample agenda you might use to provide some structure to this meeting.

Sample Supplier-Team Agenda

1) Summarize the purpose of the meeting: "To put together a plan to improve our efficiency by working on 'do more of/do less of' ideas."

2) Review the "do more of" data you've collected. Ask if anyone wants to add another item. Check to make sure everyone understands each item.

3) Prioritize the "do more of" items the group will work on by deciding which has the highest payoff for the least effort.

4) Develop a list of steps required to take action on your high-priority "do more of" items. Make sure you identify who will do what by when.

5) Repeat the above steps for the "do less of" items.

Getting in Touch with Your Customers

In the previous section we talked about getting to know your internal suppliers and their requirements. Now it's time to look at your customers—the people, departments, and work groups you supply with products and services.

Think about this: What single element is most responsible for the demise of vaudeville and the Studebaker? They were out of touch with their customers! Not only would your team not want to go the way of "classics" like the vinyl LP, but you can make your work easier by staying in closer contact with your customers. Can you think of an example in your company of someone losing touch with his or her customers? Here's one from an auto manufacturer.

"We couldn't believe it. When we actually started talking to our dealers, we found out that the reports we spent up to four hours a week putting together were typically thrown out by the dealers. They contained no real useful information!"

How can you get better connected with your customers? Begin by evaluating the sources of information your team already has about customer needs and reactions.

List the sources of customer information your team has now:	Is this source *timely?* 0 = Never 1 = Yearly 2 = Monthly or quarterly 3 = Daily	Is this source *specific?* 1 = No, only ratings 2 = Moderately (some comments) 3 = Very (extensive comments)	Does this source come *directly* to the team? 0 = Only by word of mouth 1 = No, we have to ask for it 2 = Someone else gives it to us 3 = Yes, we get it first
Example: Customer complaint report	0 The team never actually sees this report; it only goes to sales.	2	0 We get info only by word of mouth—even if we ask for the report. Total Score: 2
			Total Score:
			Total Score:

Improving Your Sources

Give yourself a total score for each source of customer information. You'll need to take action to improve any scores below 6. Here are some tips on how to do that.

If your sources score low on timeliness, try:

- Asking the customer for more frequent feedback. Customers are often willing to do this if they trust you to make improvements based on their feedback. If you haven't reached this level of trust with your customers, you might want to suggest a trial period for receiving feedback more frequently.

- Using an abbreviated method for collecting feedback that's relatively easy for the customer. For example, instead of asking customers to fill out a survey, you could call them and do a brief phone survey.

If your sources score low on being specific, try:

- Making the method interactive (talking to the customer on the phone, visiting the customer's site, having the customer visit your operation, etc.). This will allow you time to ask follow-up questions and to be sure you understand the feedback.

- Revising the questions or prompts used to collect feedback. The customer feedback process might have been designed by someone who doesn't understand what information your team needs.

- Making it easy for the customer to give you complete information (by giving your customers an 800 number, your team's voice mail number, etc.).

If your sources don't come directly to the team, try:

- Meeting with the person or group who first receives the information to explain how getting it more directly (talking with the customer face-to-face, receiving report data immediately, etc.) would benefit the team. This does not need to be a case of your team receiving the information *instead* of the other party—you're just asking to be included when the information is distributed.

- Automating the feedback system so that your team doesn't have to wait for intracompany mail.

Customer Feedback Systems Other Teams Have Tried

In a quandary about what type of feedback system your team should use? Consider these examples:

- Some teams use a system in which each feedback form returned by a customer serves as a lottery ticket, with one winner each quarter. The team rewards the winning customer with a free product or service.

- Other team members give their business cards to customers and encourage them to call whenever there's a problem.

- Some team members each "adopt" a customer and call that person regularly to get feedback.

Gathering Speed: Negotiating with Your Customers

Notes. . .

Slowly but surely your team has forged ahead and is beginning to mesh as a unit. (The boat not only floats—it's self-propelled!) You've been working hard to get better connected with your customers and suppliers. By now you know something about customers' requirements and how meeting their needs can help your team achieve its goals. This month your team will continue to focus on customers; you'll learn how to negotiate agreements with them and build the team's stamina to make customer focus a permanent part of your team's daily business. Most teams start by working with their internal customers and then apply what they've learned to their dealings with external customers.

Negotiating Agreements with Internal Customers

The lines between internal and external customers are becoming increasingly blurred these days. Your team might come in one day to discover that an internal customer's function has been "outsourced" and—poof!—suddenly you have an *external* customer. The trick, of course, is to treat all of your customers with respect and respond to their needs. Some of them just happen to be a bit closer and (allegedly) more accessible.

Whether your customers are internal or external, one of the keys to getting your customers what they want when they want it is to ask questions (see the next page). And if a customer is asking for something you're not sure the team can provide, you'll need to negotiate and agree on an arrangement that's suitable to all.

The Four Factors of Customer Agreements

Anytime you're negotiating with customers, there are four important factors to consider:

- Quantity—**how many** do they want?

- Schedule—**when** do they want it?

- Characteristics—**what features** do they need?

- Resources—**what do you need** to produce it?

These factors are interrelated so closely that it's difficult to change one without affecting the other three. Unfortunately, many new teams fall into the trap of agreeing to a change in one factor (such as delivering 20 percent more cellular razzmatazzes) without considering the impact it could have on the others (such as lengthening the schedule, dropping a time-consuming feature, or paying for more resources). You can avoid this trap by using the worksheet on the right to help work out balanced, realistic agreements with your customers.

Negotiating a Balanced Agreement

What changes have customers asked your team to make?	Which of the four factors will be affected?	What can you suggest to reach a more balanced agreement?	How would you approach the customer?
Sample: The customer wants to receive the shipment four days earlier than usual.	Directly: Schedule Indirectly: It could affect quantity, characteristics, or resources.	We could work overtime to get it out and charge more (resources); we could send a partial shipment now and the rest later (quantity); we could ship the materials without the binders (characteristics).	1) Make sure the customer understands the importance of the four factors. 2) Ask the customer to decide which of the other factors can slip. 3) Offer the team's suggestions.

Searching for Specifics

Another potential stumbling block for new teams is the vague requirement. Often teams think they know what the customer wants, but really don't. This usually results in a lot of wasted effort.

Keeping the four factors in mind, use the following questions when talking with customers to help clarify their requirements:

Quantity:

- How many do you need?

- How do you need them delivered?

Schedule:

- When do you need final delivery?

- Are there any interim milestones?

- How will we measure progress at the milestones?

Characteristics:

- What physical features do you need?

- What operational features do you need?

- What reliability/durability features do you need?

- What serviceability features do you need?

Resources:

- How much flexibility is there on price?

- Does it matter how we use our resources to meet the requirements?

Staying Focused

As with many good intentions (exercise programs, home-improvement projects, New Year's resolutions), it's often easier to start something than it is to sustain any kind of concerted effort. Such is the fate of many customer-focused initiatives; they start strong and yield promising results, but soon the energy and enthusiasm fizzle out. And when we're talking about losing touch with customers' needs, we face the business equivalent of running with scissors: Something bad is going to happen; you just don't know when.

To assess your team's customer-focus stamina, check your responses to the following statements.

Team Stamina: The Staying-with-It Factor

	SA	A	U	D	SD
1. Compared to other teams, we tend to stick with new plans or ideas longer.					
2. Of the ideas we agreed to last year, more than 75 percent are still being actively supported by the team.					
3. We're better at coming up with ideas than implementing them.					
4. We're good at making lists, but we hardly ever refer to them.					
5. We tend to take on more than we can reasonably handle as a team.					
6. If someone on the team misses a deadline or doesn't keep a commitment, it's usually no big deal.					
7. The average time span for our team to remain excited about something is less than three months.					
8. If a project lasts longer than three months, our team tends to lose interest.					
9. We are very disciplined in using lists to follow up on action items and agreements.					
10. We get more satisfaction from generating ideas than implementing them.					

Key

SA = Strongly Agree   **A** = Agree   **U** = Undecided   **D** = Disagree   **SD** = Strongly Disagree

Scoring:

For items 1, 2, and 9:   **SA**=5, **A**=4, **U**=3,
                          D=2, **SD**=1

For items 3, 4, 5, 6, 7, 8,
and 10:   **SA**=1, **A**=2, **U**=3,
                          D=4, **SD**=5

Add your scores and use the scale at the right to assess your team's customer focus.

If your team scored between:

10–25—Your team has a serious problem with follow-through; select and implement at least five ideas from the list on the next page.

25–35—Your team has an average level of follow-through skill; select and implement at least three ideas from the list on the next page.

35–50—Your team does better than most in the area of follow-through, but you should probably select at least one idea on the next page for good measure.

Check the ideas you plan to use.

Ideas to Keep Your Customer Focus

☐ Start each team meeting with feedback from your customers—just to make sure it doesn't get lost in the shuffle.

☐ Make customer satisfaction or meeting customer expectations your team's number one goal.

☐ Arrange regular, ongoing visits with your customers. Many teams rotate this responsibility among team members because it can be such a powerful experience to see how customers use your product or service.

☐ Invite customers to your operation at least once a year. Use this as an opportunity to discuss their changing requirements and the improvements your team has made based on their feedback.

☐ Ask each team member to "adopt" a customer by calling them regularly and helping them resolve problems.

☐ Each quarter, target one customer with whom the team has been having difficulties. Form a special "SWAT" team to resolve those problems.

☐ Develop a two- or three-year customer-satisfaction plan with short- and long-term objectives.

Keep Your Leader Informed

Making Decisions and Handling Work Habits Issues as a Team

Notes. . .

Your team has progressed to the point where you can focus on refining and improving many of your processes and work patterns. When the team started out, you handled things as best you could, just to get them done. In fact, your first meetings probably were pretty rough. And unless you stop to reexamine what you're doing, some of those early, choppy work patterns can become habits that eventually will get in the way. So now is a good time to take a fresh look at some of your team processes. Chances are your team is ready to progress to more sophisticated ways of working. In this month we'll look at two important team skills: decision making and handling poor work habits.

Shoring Up Team Decision Making

One of the team processes most susceptible to bad habits is decision making. After 10 months of working in teams, you've certainly seen some of the Six Deadly Patterns of Gaining Agreement.

1. **Stinking Rethinking**—When, after finally agreeing on something, a team member reopens the issue, and the group rehashes the whole enchilada—only to reach the original conclusion.

2. **GroupThink**—When the team agrees on a course of action that no one really wants because people aren't willing to say what they really think.

3. **Premature Closure**—When someone in the team shuts off further discussion before all the important issues have been explored.

4. **Swirling and Twirling**—When the team never reaches agreement. Members bring up issues that are discussed and left hanging without any concrete action plan.

5. **Pompous Pontificating**—When a team member (often a repeat offender) talks at great length, and everyone else tunes out.

6. **Teamocentric Thinking**—When the team fails to include other key stakeholders in the decision-making process (forgetting about anyone outside the team).

The Six Deadly Patterns can produce a diverse range of effects, from the merely annoying (everyone rolls their eyes as a team member launches off on a tangent) to the decidedly disastrous (the Cuban Missile Crisis is a classic example of GroupThink).

Unfortunately, these patterns can sneak up on you and become so ingrained that the team doesn't even realize it. So, to heighten your awareness, we've included a checklist of symptoms. You can use it to determine if your team is stuck in any of these patterns. Check the column under the letter(s) that best describes how you feel about each statement.

Team Decision-Making Checklist

Stinking Rethinking

	SA	A	U	D	SD
1. When even one person misses a meeting, we have to rehash and reconsider decisions the team made.					
2. We often rehash decisions we made weeks or months ago.					

GroupThink

	SA	A	U	D	SD
1. In meetings or discussions we have difficulty saying what we really think.					
2. Sometimes we agree on a course of action that some team members know is wrong.					

Premature Closure

	SA	A	U	D	SD
1. We tend to push for agreement before everyone has had a say.					
2. Disagreement about a course of action is most likely to come up after the team meeting.					

Key

SA = Strongly Agree   **A** = Agree   **U** = Undecided   **D** = Disagree   **SD** = Strongly Disagree

Swirling and Twirling

1. We often carry over agenda items from one meeting to the next.

2. We have difficulty "nailing things down" to a solid action plan; even after long discussions, it's difficult to tell who's supposed to do what.

Pompous Pontificating

1. We have at least one team member who takes up more than 20 percent of the "airtime" in our meetings.

2. People automatically tune out certain members because they are known windbags.

Teamocentric Thinking

1. We often get feedback from our leader or other groups that we overlooked important information from others outside the team.

2. We rarely bring up the customer when we're making decisions.

	SA	A	U	D	SD

Interpreting the Checklist

If you agreed or strongly agreed with two items in any one category, your team has a serious problem with that decision-making pattern. If you agreed or strongly agreed with more than six items in the entire checklist, your team needs to work on its general processes for reaching agreement.

What You Can Do

Here are some tips to improve your team's decision making:

- Appoint a special "decision referee" to watch for symptoms of the Six Deadly Patterns.

- Use a Team Decision-Making Checklist before finalizing agreements to be sure you've included all the key perspectives.

- Continue to evaluate the quality of the team's decision-making processes.

Dealing with Team Members' Annoying Work Habits

Coming in late. Leaving the work area a mess. Interrupting you when you're trying to get work done. Making too much noise just when the team needs some quiet. It happens to every team at one time or another: a member whose technical performance is fine, but whose sloppy work habits are driving everybody off the deep end.

Ironically, it's often easier to deal with true performance problems (team members who don't produce the necessary quality or quantity of work). Most organizations track performance indicators closely and have programs, policies, and procedures to deal with poor performance. It can be more difficult to address someone's annoying habits or behaviors because these issues are more subjective (for example, one person's mess is another person's natural state) and can be highly personal (for instance, one team had to deal with someone's body odor problem).

Because most of us aren't comfortable providing constructive feedback to others, the typical scenario goes something like this:

Stage 1—You stew about the problem until you can't stand it anymore (this stage often involves useless complaining to spouses or pets; they don't understand and can't do anything about the problem). This stage soon slips into:

Stage 2—You complain to coworkers about the problem. (And the longer this stage goes on, the greater the likelihood that the subject of your complaints will find out about them and feel outraged that everyone is talking behind his or her back.) This eventually leads to:

Stage 3—Your complaining to coworkers hasn't resolved the problem, and surprisingly no one has volunteered to speak to the offending party. So when you've reached the end of your rope, you either blow up at the person in question or give up in disgust and ask your leader to deal with it.

A Better Way . . .

A much better way to handle this sort of thing is to deal with the aggravating work habit while it's a molehill and before it interferes with your mental health or the team's cohesiveness.

Here's an approach that should help your team handle these kinds of problems:

1. As soon as you become aware of the problem, speak directly to the offending team member. (See the guidelines on the next page to help with this discussion.)

2. If there's no improvement, discuss the problem in general in a team meeting ("Our production schedule dipped last month for several reasons, one of which was people coming in late. . . .") and reinforce or establish team norms for acceptable behavior.

3. If the problem still isn't corrected, you'll have to resort to your organization's formal policies. These might include peer review or taking the issue to your leader, but at least you'll have given the offending team member ample feedback and opportunity to improve (which would be important to you if you were on the receiving end in this sort of situation).

When You Have to Confront Someone . . .

Often it's helpful to think through this kind of discussion beforehand, so you're able to make your point in a way that doesn't damage your relationship with another team member. Use the guidelines and example on the facing page to help plan your discussion.

A Better Way to Confront Someone

	Guidelines	Example	Your Situation
1.	Describe the work habit you've observed.	"Lately a lot of your calls have been switched over to me because you've been taking personal calls."	
2.	Indicate why it concerns you.	"I can't always answer your customers' questions as well as you can."	
3.	Ask for your team member's perspective and listen openly to the explanation.	"This has never been an issue before, and I wanted to see if everything was OK. . . ."	
4.	Ask for ideas for addressing the problem.	"What do you think we can do about this?"	
5.	Summarize agreements.	"So you'll make those calls over breaks, or check with me in advance if your calls are going to be rolling over to me?"	

If you discuss these problems early on, it can help keep your team running smoothly. If you ignore them, even one team member's bad habit can create friction in your group and ruin the whole team's morale.

Picking Up Speed: Managing Your Time

Notes. . .

After months of hard work, the team should be getting stronger. Increased energy, a variety of more-refined skills, and a sharper focus all will enable you to make significant strides. Unwanted, energy-sapping team conflicts are a thing of the past, and people are comfortable with the team's processes. You've also probably noticed that the team is more focused on external challenges than internal issues. This external focus will help the team expand its horizons and become more open to learning from others.

Barriers to Learning

As you move from an us-versus-them mentality, there are several attitudes that can get in the way of a team's development and learning:

- **NIH** (Not Invented Here) **Syndrome—** This is the universal tendency of teams to reject ideas from other teams or individuals. If you find yourself or team members saying

things like, "That'll never work here," or "Our team is unique," you might be caught in the throes of NIH. When a team is first forming, NIH serves a useful purpose: It helps the team build internal cohesiveness. But if you wallow too long in NIH, the team will start to stagnate.

- **BINOF** (But It's Not Our Fault)—Many teams' instinctive reaction to any mistake or problem is to cover their collective butt—often by deflecting the blame onto others. (One team was so skillful at this that they became known as the Teflon™ Team because nothing could stick to them.) The downside here is that all the energy that goes into deflection could be better spent analyzing root causes of the error or breakdown and using that information to improve team processes. Even when the team's process is not the cause, if team performance suffers, the team needs to be involved in getting up to speed (which isn't likely to happen if people are busy setting up their deflector shields).

- **BWADITW** (But We've Always Done It This Way)—This is a natural defense mechanism a lot of team members use in the early stages of team formation to prevent the sheer volume of change from overwhelming them. But it's time to move beyond this. The team should be emotionally ready to consider new ways of working.

Once you get beyond these barriers to learning, there are many rich sources of information the team can use to pick up new ideas. Here are a few:

- **The successes of other teams.** You can mine this source by: "trading" a successful technique with another team; scheduling a team open house where all the teams share learning experiences; or targeting a specific team that is good at something that you need to improve.

- **Your own mistakes.** The best teams treat their mistakes as learning opportunities. Instead of trying to cover up your snafus, discuss them in team meetings and make a log of them to use when training new members. Generally, find ways to prevent them from happening again.

- **Benchmarking.** It's a good idea to identify other teams' best practices and find ways to adapt them to your situation. With so much information available, it's even possible to conduct "armchair" research by reading about other teams' practices (you don't even have to leave the comfort of your own work area). You might want to assign team members to read and report on new ideas; then, at team meetings, choose an idea to try.

Team Time Management

Sometimes teams don't take time to analyze mistakes or learn from them because they're too busy trying to cover all of their newfound responsibilities.

Does it sometimes feel like your life is out of control, especially since you joined the team? For many new team members, there seems to be more to do and less time to do it. If you don't take control of this situation, you'll soon feel like a hamster on its exercise wheel: running faster and faster, but never getting anywhere.

Are You Out of Control?

Try this simple survey to determine whether you need to get your time under control. Check the appropriate column after each statement and then total your score.

	SA	A	U	D	SD
	5	4	3	2	1

1. I have to juggle more things at work than ever before.

2. For the first time in my life, I'm starting to miss deadlines and forget my commitments.

3. I can never seem to find time to do my team assignments.

4. I often have to stay late or take work home to get it all done.

5. I have a difficult time breaking away from work to do my team assignments.

Total Score:

Key

SA = Strongly Agree   **A** = Agree   **U** = Undecided   **D** = Disagree   **SD** = Strongly Disagree

Interpreting Your Score

If your total score is 10 or less, you should become a time-management missionary and bring help to the less fortunate. If you scored between 11 and 17, you are in the normal range and would experience relief by using some of the suggestions on the following pages. If your score is between 18 and 25, you need to implement the suggestions on the next page and ask for coaching (before you sink further into a time abyss) from someone who has learned to manage time effectively.

Suggestions for Team Time Management

You probably do have more responsibilities than you did before teams. Many people get accustomed to knowing exactly what to expect every day. They slide into a routine, concentrating solely on the technical aspect of their job. With teams there's more variety; people have to get information from other areas, meet with different people, and keep track of more things. They might even need to spend more time out of their own work area than they ever did before. To the new team member, these strange new duties can seem very overwhelming—even impossible.

Don't despair! You, too, can learn to manage your time with the best of them. Here are a few rules to live by:

- **Balance!** Many new team members continue to view the technical aspects of the job as their "real work"; their team responsibilities become "extras" to be squeezed in. Big mistake! If you take this approach, you'll be doomed to Eternal Frustration. It's better to estimate what percentage of your time will be spent on team activities (meetings, projects, assignments, etc.) and then plan to make it happen. Many organizations estimate that team activities will take 10–30 percent of employees' time. With that in mind, you can clear time in your schedule by: tossing overboard non-value-adding responsibilities, asking team members to cover for you, and sharing responsibilities with team members.

- **Prioritize.** We've already established that it probably will be impossible to do everything you're asked to do. For the first time in your career, you might need to practice saying "no" and prioritizing your remaining tasks. The personal and team goals that you set in New Team Month 4 should be the best gauge for determining how important something really is.

A Case in Point

Consider the case of Darlene, an accounts payable analyst on a financial services team. Darlene had always taken pride in getting things done and enjoyed her reputation as a hard worker. When her organization converted to teams, Darlene became her team's administrative coordinator. That meant scheduling team meetings, tracking attendance, and calling in temporary help when the team's workload was heavy. She tackled these new responsibilities with characteristic gusto.

Soon though, Darlene realized things were slipping. She regularly took the absenteeism report home. And team members complained when she arranged for extra help; they resented having to cover her phone while Darlene spent up to an hour trying to get a temp. It wasn't long before Darlene had to admit not only that she was miserable, but that she wasn't as on top of her job as she used to be.

So instead of doing the absenteeism report one night, Darlene thought about how she could regain control over her work. She started by buying a planner to track her commitments and stay better organized. The planner helped Darlene evaluate her activities against the goals she had set with the team at the beginning of the year. This exercise made it clear that at least two activities (the Annual Picnic Committee and the time-tracking charts) weren't contributing one bit to achieving team or personal goals. Darlene acted quickly: She dropped out of the committee and found a way to reduce time tracking to half an hour each month.

Darlene also recognized the root problem of leaving the work area to call in temp help: It was too unpredictable. Her team members never knew when Darlene's calls might be forwarded to them. To eliminate the uncertainty, Darlene set up a rotating schedule of standby coverage from 8–9 a.m.; the designated standby member could plan his or her workload to allow for the possibility of picking up Darlene's calls. Darlene also learned to use the team to help her prioritize.

In the case of the time-consuming absenteeism report, Darlene asked the team to decide which was more important: spending time on the absenteeism report or typing and distributing the minutes from each meeting. The team helped Darlene find a way to reduce the time she spent on both activities.

Darlene and her planner lived happily ever after.

- **Organize.** Many teams maintain a "Team To-Do List" with all the actions prioritized and clearly marked with who is responsible for doing what by when. Even though many computer software packages offer this handy feature, you don't have to do it electronically. You can simply post a handwritten list in your team area; that way, it's easy to see at a glance who's overwhelmed or overcommitted.

Team Time Management Tricks

The suggestions you just read are a must for any effective time manager. Here are some tricks to make it easier for you to control your time.

- Use the power of the team. One person can't be in two places at once, but a team can! When one team member is temporarily swamped, other members can pitch in. Some teams ask members to post a "burnout rating" when they log on to the computer system each day. That way other team members can offer help and support.

- Ask the team to help you prioritize. If the team asks you to take on a new task, ask for help in deciding what you're not going to do or what you can put on the back burner.

- Post a team calendar and to-do list where everyone can see it.

- Document what's worked well so you don't waste time trying to recreate what you already know is effective.

- Periodically check how the team is spending its time based on the roles you defined in the New Team Development Phase. Are you spending enough time in personal development and special projects, or are you back in your old role?

Taking Initiative as a Team

Notes. . .

Month 13

Let's face it—teams have personalities just like people do. Some are very positive and upbeat; others drown in a sea of chronic dissatisfaction. Some are very task oriented; others like to have a good time while they work. And some are gung ho while others are slugs. This last description can be crucial. The amount of initiative a team demonstrates in solving problems and capitalizing on opportunities can be pivotal to its success or failure.

Gung Ho or Slug?

How much initiative does your team have? Use the checklist below to help you find out. Check any statement that applies to you or your team.

Gung Ho	**Slug**
☐ We have several continuous improvement projects going on at once.	☐ We still haven't started any significant improvement projects.
☐ More than 75 percent of the team is actively engaged in improvement projects right now.	☐ More than 50 percent of the team really doesn't care and isn't actively engaged in anything beyond their immediate work.
☐ The team often suggests new ideas to management.	☐ We wait for management to tell us what to do.
☐ We've developed new ways of doing things; other teams have followed our lead.	☐ We haven't even adopted new processes that other teams are already using.
☐ We get so excited when we're working on a new idea that we often put in extra hours in the rush to get it done.	☐ We rarely get excited about anything—certainly not enough to put in extra hours.

How to Jump-Start a Sluggish Team

If you checked more than one item in the "Slug" column, there are some tricks you can use to get moving and maintain that momentum. Review the following list of suggestions and check any that you might be able to use with your team.

☐ Set a goal of considering one new idea per team meeting.

☐ Appoint an "initiatives coordinator" within the team—someone to stimulate new projects and approaches.

☐ Run a contest within the team for "Best Initiative" or "Initiator of the Month."

☐ Swap member(s) with a high-initiative team for a month to get a fresh infusion of ideas and energy.

☐ Set up a board to track team initiatives.

☐ Ask your leader for ideas on what the team could do to take more initiative.

☐ Do a force field analysis to see what's preventing the team from taking initiative; try to remove one barrier each week. (If you're not familiar with a force field diagram, the idea is to chart organizational pressures that [in this case] aid or impede the team's initiative. Draw a series of opposing arrows [representing forces at work in the organization] and label each.) Keep all the "aiding" forces on the same side; likewise, the "impeding" forces. This type of diagram should give you a good idea of the barriers you're facing.

Aiding Forces | Impeding Forces

Pitfalls for Maturing Teams

If your efforts to spark initiative are falling flat and the team is still sluggish, you might be facing a more serious problem. Ironically, sometimes the very factors that helped you mature and succeed as a team can trip you up in the long haul. Teams that have been working together a long time are prone to certain "diseases" at this stage of their development. Be on the lookout for:

- **Burnout.** This occurs when it feels as if there's no energy or enthusiasm left in the team. Tension, overwork, frustration, and lack of focus all contribute to burnout.

- **Complacency.** This often happens when the team has worked very hard for an extended period and decides to come up for air. If the "rest break" is prolonged, the team might have difficulty regaining its momentum.

- **Elitism.** This is the result when a team crosses the fine line between confidence and arrogance.

What About Your Team?

Review the list of pitfalls and symptoms on the next page. If your team is experiencing two or more of the symptoms for any one pitfall, try the suggested solutions.

Pitfall	Symptom	Possible Solutions
Burnout	• Everyone on the team seems too tired to go out of their way to do anything. • People have given up on fixing problems; the attitude is "it's never going to change." • No one gets excited about anything (even the team's accomplishments) anymore. • Sometimes it seems as if the team is moving in slow motion. • No one volunteers to take on anything. • Attendance at team meetings and other team activities has dropped off.	• Adjust your workload if the team simply has too much to do; be even more aggressive at eliminating non-value-adding activities. • Recharge the team by giving members new, more interesting work to do. This might mean rotating assignments sooner than you had planned or taking on new, more interesting work from your leader. • If the team needs more positive reinforcement, schedule an informal celebration (doughnut break, pizza party, etc.).
Complacency	• The team isn't interested in learning anything new; people have stopped signing up for training. • The team sets the same goals year after year. • The team hasn't changed any processes in the last four months.	• Consider bringing in someone from the outside to inject enthusiasm. (Customers or top-level leaders are great for helping the team overcome inertia; they're especially good at helping the team set new, more challenging goals.) • Involve the team in training others; you can't help but learn something new in the process.
Elitism	• The team rejects suggestions and ideas from outside the team. • The team won't admit mistakes. • The team thinks no one else is good enough to join the group. • The team spends a lot of time discussing its accomplishments. • The team refuses to ask for help from people outside the team.	• To help the team get a more-rounded view of how others perceive it, conduct anonymous surveys of customers and internal partners—with an emphasis on finding out areas for improvement. • Even if your team has a track record of high performance, you should be working on at least one area for improvement.

Development Activity: Team Fill-in-the-Blank

Introduction

In the past 13 months your team has worked hard to develop skills that will help it become a more sophisticated, cohesive unit. As you learned more about team functioning, you also became more aware of the team's needs and issues. Until now, it would've been difficult for the team to take an objective "look in the mirror." But now that the team has become more mature, it's easier to recognize problems and patterns. This is a good time to gauge just how far you've come.

In this exercise each team member will interview another team member, asking him or her to "fill in the blank" on some thought-provoking questions. The results of the interviews will be posted— without names attached—and processed by the team.

Materials

You'll need one customized interview guide for each team member and blank flip charts for each item or category.

Total Time Allotment

You'll need 20–30 minutes for each interview, 30 minutes to post interview results, and one hour to process them.

Instructions

1. The team must decide which six of the following items are most important. This can be done in a team meeting or by posting the questions and having team members vote for their top six choices. In making your selections, it's important to have a balance of items that are designed to generate positive and negative feedback.

   ☐ The thing I am proudest about on this team is . . .

   ☐ I think our team is becoming . . .

   ☐ The thing I find most frustrating about this team is . . .

   ☐ Compared to other teams, we . . .

   ☐ We are best at . . .

   ☐ Our team is having difficulty . . .

   ☐ I think our next project should be . . .

   ☐ We are avoiding . . .

   ☐ Our greatest strength is . . .

   ☐ I think we could have more fun if . . .

2. Have one team member generate a short interview guide that includes the six items selected and enough space underneath each item for notes.

3. Make interview assignments. It's best if members can interview the person on the team with whom they work least (someone whose work area isn't nearby, who has worked on different projects, etc.).

4. In a meeting area, post a flip chart for each item on the interview guide (six flip charts). Ask members to write the collected responses on the flip chart without indicating who the source of each response was.

5. Select six team members to read and interpret the answers on the charts (one team member assigned to each chart). Each team member should be prepared to complete these three statements:

☐ The trend from the answers to this item seems to be . . .

☐ There were interesting differences about . . .

☐ What we should do about this is . . .

6. The team can then do a gallery walk; that is, the entire team moves to each chart in turn, stopping to read the responses and participating in a discussion led by the team member assigned to that chart.

7. The team can wrap up the activity by putting together a complete action plan. Use the table on the right to help you.

What needs to be done	By whom	By when

Mature Team Phase

For the past 13 months your team has navigated through the unfamiliar waters of high-performance teams. You've become equipped with skills not only to survive, but to flourish. It's time to move on to new challenges. Use the activities outlined over the next few months to continue developing your team's role.

Month 1

Shifting the Focus: Are You Ready?

Month 2

Moving to the Next Level: Team Survival Tips

Month 3

What You Can Expect from Your Leader; Operating *Inter*dependently

Month 4

Broadening Your Perspective and Coping with Your Success

Month 5

Celebrating Progress; Staying Fresh and Focused

Mature Team Phase

What to Expect

You've survived doubts and awkwardness in the early stages of team development. Your team should be moving toward the fourth stage of team development: Full Speed Ahead.

4. Full Speed Ahead

1. Getting
Started

3. Getting
on Course

2. Going in
Circles

Everyone on the team should have a much more realistic, informed view of what it's like to work in teams. The advantages and the challenges are clear. And by now you and your teammates understand one another's differences and have learned to work together effectively.

Possible Concerns

Sometimes I think our team is getting stale. We know one another really well—sometimes too well. We can guess what people are going to say before they say it, and we know who's going to volunteer before even asking for one. I think we've started to make assumptions about one another—without even bothering to ask what the others might want. How can we get out of this rut?

Many mature teams are in the same boat; unfortunately, not all of them recognize it. The problem is that teams and individual team members often get typecast in specific roles. Case in point: Because early in the team's formation Bob turned down a chance to learn the new computerized scheduling system, he was never again asked to do anything with the computer. This became like a vicious tropical storm that was never downgraded. When Bob figured that no one trusted him to do any computer work, he lost confidence and started avoiding the computer even more, which reinforced everyone's initial stereotypes.

To avoid this trap, the team needs to make a conscious effort to "stretch" as a team and as individuals. For example, one accounts payable team felt bogged down and uninspired after working together for 18 months, so they decided to ask the "Cruise Director" (the team member responsible for team morale and development) to shake things up.

The Cruise Director helped the team:

- Set "personal challenge" goals each year. (One team member's biggest fear was public speaking, so she set a goal to speak for 10 minutes in front of at least one visiting group before the end of the year.)

- Distribute action items at the end of each meeting not according to who *has* the most experience, but according to who *needs* the most experience.

Shifting the Focus: Are You Ready?

Notes. . .

Have you ever been on a long car trip with anyone under the age of 14? If so, you've heard The Question: "Are we there yet?" (usually delivered in the kind of ear-splitting, nasal whine that makes you wonder why you ever left home in the first place). And if your answer was "No," you probably heard something like, "I can't stand it anymore! I can't wait to get out of this car!"

Sometimes being part of a team that has beached and can't get going can be a lot like one of those dreaded car trips. The best way to maintain your sanity (besides daydreams of a Caribbean cruise) is to keep yourself challenged and amused. This means evolving as a team, with members continuing to take on new roles while shedding their old ones. It means moving to the next level: a mature team.

Shifting the Focus

When you first heard about this "team stuff," your focus was mainly (and quite naturally) on yourself. Once the team formed, that focus shifted to the team (how to get along and work with everyone with minimal bloodshed). Now that the team is maturing, you can shift the focus again—to larger organizational and business issues. To check how far your thinking has evolved, see the chart on the next page.

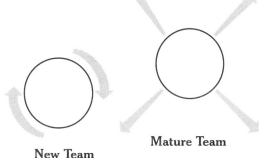

Preteam

New Team

Mature Team

	Preteam	New Team	Mature Team
Focus	What is happening to me?	What is happening in the team?	What is happening in the organization?
Tasks	Learning about the vision and direction for teams. Developing basic skills for working together.	Working out team operating guidelines. Working on improving team performance and operating efficiency.	Working on improving customer performance and satisfaction. Taking full responsibility for managing the team.
Personal Concerns	What is going to happen to me? How will my job change?	How am I fitting in with the team? How do I like working with the other team members? How are we going to work together? How can we agree on things? How can we handle these new responsibilities?	What other opportunities are out there? What's next for us?
Team Issues	(There is no team yet.)	How are we going to work together? How can we agree on things? How can we handle these new responsibilities?	How can we continue to advance?
Development Priorities	Learning what teams are and how they work.	Learning skills for working effectively with others in a team.	Learning about the business as a whole to make more-advanced improvements.

Are You Ready?

Moving to the next level might cause some anxious moments for you or your teammates. Are you and the team ready for the transition to mature teams? Use the following checklists to find out.

You

☐ You are competent in the following skills:

- Leading a team meeting.
- Facilitating a team decision.
- Resolving interpersonal conflict within the team.
- Training and coaching others.

☐ You can perform 60 percent of the jobs on the team.

☐ You have competently handled several tasks forwarded by the leader.

☐ You have come out of your "silo" focus and can work anywhere in the team.

The Team

☐ The team consistently meets its goals.

☐ The team has resolved most of its major internal conflicts.

☐ The team no longer sees everything in "us-versus-them" terms; it recognizes interdependencies with other groups.

Moving to the Next Level: Team Survival Tips

Notes. . .

Your team has navigated through the stormiest of seas and is poised to rise to the next level of performance. How can you make sure that neither you nor the team belly flops? Let's look at how you can use the Team Survival Tips to your advantage.

Team Survival Tips

1. **Become a quick-change artist.** Your role is continuing to evolve—it's important that you keep pace with changes that might affect your team. You want to avoid the fate of some team members who inadvertently became mired in the New Team Stage—focusing on the team's internal issues—and never graduated to working on interteam or more strategic business issues. Can you think of any changes that might affect your team? How can you prepare for them? Use the space on the right to help organize your thoughts.

Changes to expect	What you must do to prepare
Develop a broader business focus.	
Concentrate more on issues outside the team.	
Work more on big-picture problems.	
Become even more self-managed.	

2. **Add value.** Your ability to understand and contribute to the larger business can greatly increase your value as an employee. As the team matures, you'll need to focus on making cross-team improvements, streamlining the supplier chain, and producing measurable results for customers. You'll find that you're increasingly gauging your impact—not on results that occur within the team (increased productivity, lower absenteeism), but on results *for your customers* (on-time delivery, customer satisfaction, etc.). Use the space on the right to list the measures you now use to gauge your (and the team's) effectiveness and the measures you'll use in the future.

Measures you use now to gauge your/the team's effectiveness	Measures you'll need to use in the future

3. **Take ownership for yourself and the company.** Now that you've had considerable experience working in teams, you might want to reconsider your career options. This is one of the great advantages of working in teams: You're aware of a much greater variety of options than you would be in a traditional structure.

    By this time your team experience should have allowed you to "sample" the work from other parts of the organization. Case in point: After 18 months in a field service team, one team member moved to a technical position in planning (the department with which he had been the team liaison), and another took a team leadership position in another part of the organization. Now is the time to decide in which areas you could contribute the most. Use the space on the right to help you identify possible career options.

Possible career options that interest you	What you need to do to find out about each option

4. **Become a lifelong learner.** Development in the Mature Team Phase focuses more on understanding the business and the environment in which the team operates. Depending on your career interests, you can learn more about any of a number of new opportunities, including (see if one of these fits) a functional area that interests you, project management skills, the requirements of a particular group of customers, or the costs and efficiencies of your supplier network. The learning possibilities are almost limitless. Here are some guidelines to focus your thinking:

    - List some learning opportunities that you'd like to get involved with.

    - Rank the opportunities in order of interest to you.

    - Identify two things you could do to get more information about these opportunities.

5. **Manage your own morale.** In the Mature Team Phase most people derive job satisfaction from different sources than they did before. As they develop a better understanding of the broader business, many team members enjoy being "mini entrepreneurs." They develop their own ideas, evaluate costs and benefits, and even carry their ideas through implementation. Others enjoy more customer contact or learning more about other parts of the organization. As one team member said:

    "Finance was always a mystery to me. It seemed like our team cost reports went into a big black hole. When I actually started working with one of the analysts on a project, I was fascinated. Now I'm enrolled in our company's Finance for Nonfinancial People course, and I'm thinking of revising some of the team's cost reporting."

6. **Monitor your own expectations.** Don't expect to start sailing along at this point. It might feel as if you've been battling some fierce gusts for awhile. And it might be tempting to kick back and enjoy the gentle lap of the waves as they move you along your course. Resist this temptation—or you'll find yourself against the wind again. The advantages of getting to the Mature Team Stage come from being able to navigate in new directions—not from taking a rest break.

    Identify three hopes or expectations you have for the Mature Team Phase:

    1)

    2)

    3)

    Discuss these with your team members at your next meeting.

7. **Yell for what you need.** Many companies don't plan for ongoing training, or they're not sure what kind of development mature teams need. As in earlier stages, you'll need to be clear about your personal needs and the team's needs. Chances are that the organization won't be able to anticipate that your team needs new kinds of reports on supplier performance or needs training in developing and distributing customer surveys.

    It's up to you and the team to look at the tasks and new initiatives you're planning and ask for help (in the form of training, information, introductions and contacts, time, or whatever else you need). Use the space on the next page to list any new tasks and the help you'll need to carry them out effectively.

New tasks/responsibilities	What you/the team needs to be more effective at these new tasks/responsibilities

Notes. . .

What You Can Expect from Your Leader; Operating *Inter*dependently

Notes. . .

Month 3

What to Expect from Your Leader

By now you've probably realized that your team's leader is less and less involved in the team's daily operations. Why, then, should you care what's going on with the leader? You certainly don't need a leader at this point, right? Wrong!

One of the most difficult and frustrating lessons teams learn goes something like this:

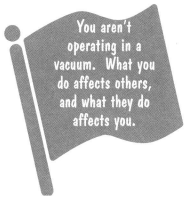

You aren't operating in a vacuum. What you do affects others, and what they do affects you.

This is particularly true of the relationship between the team and its leader. As the team becomes more self-sufficient, the leader picks up new responsibilities and is, therefore, no longer as available to the team. The more responsibilities the leader takes on, the more the team picks up in order to manage itself.

Consider the following example from one hospital care unit team.

New Team Phase	Mature Team Phase
Leader's Responsibilities • Facilitate team meetings. • Complete labor-hour report. • Ensure adequate staffing levels. • Arbitrate quality disputes. • Monitor the team's budget. • Provide coaching on cross-training. • Provide final performance feedback. • Determine pay increases.	**Leader's Responsibilities** • Lead supplier certification project. • Attend community events. • Provide coaching on placing patients in coordination with other units. • Provide final performance feedback. • Determine pay increases.
Team's Responsibilities • Cross-train in most team functions. • Post and track team performance. • Lead parts of team meetings. • Monitor clinical best practices. • Make technical process improvements. • Complete attendance report.	**Team's Responsibilities** • Facilitate team meetings. • Ensure adequate staffing levels. • Monitor team's budget. • Post and track team performance. • Make technical process improvements in conjunction with other units.
Implications • Team members have more to do. • Team leader will not attend every meeting.	**How We Need to Operate Differently** • Identify more non-value-adding tasks. • Reassign tasks. • Team leader must debrief the team about the status of his or her new tasks. • Establish new team norm that the leader attends every other meeting.

This might seem like a very organized, smooth transition; often it is. Unfortunately, it's not always that easy. Sometimes the leader withdraws from day-to-day team operations faster than the team can take on his or her duties. And sometimes the team is ready for more autonomy before the leader is ready to move on to new responsibilities. Synchronizing this change is trickier than it might appear.

To ensure that the team and your leader agree on what to expect, complete the worksheet on the right for your own situation.

Once your team and the leader have sorted out who will do what in the Mature Team Phase, a logical next step is learning to work more interdependently with other departments. The next section will give you some tips on how to do that.

Your Situation in the New Team Phase	Your Situation in the Mature Team Phase
Leader's Responsibilities	**Leader's Responsibilities**
Team's Responsibilities	**Team's Responsibilities** (What key decisions must the team make in the next two months of the Mature Team Phase? Who is responsible for these decisions?)
Implications	**How We Need to Operate Differently**

Planning to Operate More Interdependently

Most teams work through a fairly predictable process of growth: starting out fairly dependent (relying heavily on a leader's help), becoming counter-dependent (with a tendency to reject help or direction), and working up to being independent (trying not to rely on anybody outside the team).

The best teams take this process one step further: They become *interdependent*. They recognize how much they must rely on others to achieve peak performance. Instead of trying to maximize their own effectiveness (often at the expense of other teams), truly mature teams work with others to maximize the effectiveness of the entire system.

Case in point: A distribution team in a grocery products distribution company realized they had extra pallets of grocery products. The team contacted the accounting group, which helped develop a proposal for selling the additional products to customers outside the company.

The distribution team soon had a successful enterprise going. By working interdependently within the company, the distribution team was able to pull in additional revenue for the company.

Independent or Interdependent?

Is your team independent or interdependent? Use the table on the right to find out where your team is in this evolutionary process.

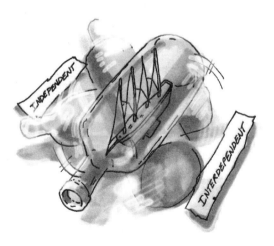

Category	Independent	Interdependent
Communications	• At least 75 percent of our communications occur within the team (among team members).	• At least 50 percent of our communications occur with key stakeholders outside the team.
Performance Measures	• Most of our measures are internal (absenteeism, productivity, number of suggestions submitted, etc.). • Most of the feedback used to rate a team member's performance comes from people inside the team.	• At least half of our measures are focused outside the team (customer satisfaction, beating competitors' quality or delivery standards, etc.). • At least 30 percent of the feedback used to rate a team member's performance comes from key customers, suppliers, and other internal or external partners.
Meetings	• Usually only members of our team attend our meetings.	• Customers, suppliers, and other internal partners routinely attend our meetings.

Actions You Can Take to Become More Interdependent

Becoming interdependent is one of your team's ultimate goals. How can you get there? Read the following suggestions and check those actions that you plan to take. Use the blank space in the next column to write in any others that your team might take.

☐ Make a list of key customers, suppliers, and other internal partners; identify how your team depends on them for success.

☐ Distribute responsibility for your key customers among team members; make it a practice to communicate with customers on a regular schedule.

☐ End each team meeting by agreeing on what needs to be communicated to people outside the team.

☐ Set joint goals with suppliers or customers.

☐ Make it a practice to invite one outside partner to each team meeting; this will keep your team better connected with the rest of the organization.

Other Actions You Can Take

☐

☐

☐

☐

Broadening Your Perspective and Coping with Your Success

Notes. . .

Month 4

Remember that old fable about the six blind men who had their hands on different parts of the elephant? When they were asked to describe the animal, each had a different (and often hilarious) version—none of which even vaguely conjured up an image of a pachyderm. Many teams find themselves in a similar situation: They have their hands on only one part of the organization and tend to see everything from that one viewpoint.

You and your team need to get beyond this limited perspective to think more like the owner of the elephant and less like the people charged with sweeping up behind the beast. But how do you get your arms around the whole animal? Here's an easy-to-follow, two-step approach.

Thinking Laterally

1. You can start by drawing a process map of your organization's business—everything from the point at which the customer contracts with you to the point where you deliver the product or service. Your organization's process is likely to be complex, so just stick to the core business and the major functions.

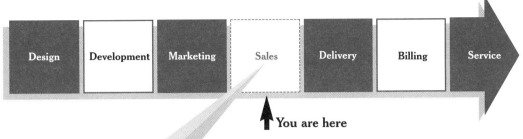

You are here

2. Then, for each step in the process, identify the functions, requirements, and issues for that part of the business. First look at the example on the right; then, keeping an internal partner group in mind, complete an example for your organization.

Sales

As you can see, understanding the big picture drops another piece of the puzzle into place for your team. Your success story is nearly complete as you reach the Mature Team Phase. Ironically, one of your final hurdles might be success itself—and how you handle it.

	Sales Example	Your Organization
What are the major functions in this area?	Account executives contact existing clients and prospects to identify their needs and convince them to use us. Sales administration determines prices and delivers training.	
How do you measure your results?	Each account executive has a sales target; these targets add up to the company sales goal of $120 million. The company also expects each territory to have 25 percent more new customers each year to maintain a 15 percent growth rate.	
What are the major problems or issues your group is facing now or will be facing in the future?	Sales are slipping because our chief competitor can deliver products 20 percent faster than we can.	
How does our group's customer service affect what you (Sales) do?	You could help us improve sales by doing anything to reduce cycle time. We have to be able to deliver orders 20 percent faster.	

Coping with Success

"Showbiz ain't all it's cracked up to be."

Elvis

We don't mean to imply that all mature teams will end up as bloated, bitter, burned-out shadows of their former selves. We're just saying that achieving success often comes with unexpected side effects. We'd like to suggest some reasonable methods of dealing with these developments.

Side Effect #1: Increased Visibility

The best teams get showcased continually. You might find yourselves becoming the Number One Stop on all tours of your organization. You might be asked to make presentations to visiting executives. Your members might be interviewed by local publications. It's the curse of success.

The critical care team in one hospital happened to be in this position. They were the first team to be formed, so it was natural that they were the most developed. Unfortunately, by the time the team figured out that they were spending 35 percent of their time on "public relations," their performance had already started to suffer.

How to cope: First of all, your team can use these opportunities to its advantage. Talking to others about your success can provide a definite boost in morale for team members; you can use these opportunities to maintain team spirit. But you might want to set individual and team limits so that these showcases don't take up more than one percent of any one member's (or five percent of the total team's) time.

Side Effect #2: Increased Responsibility

There's an old business saying that goes something like, "When there's something important to do, give it to the busiest person." The unspoken assumption is that the busiest person is the one everyone trusts and relies on; therefore, this person is the most competent. The team equivalent to this is loading more responsibility onto the team that has already taken on the most responsibility. The more capability you demonstrate, the more responsibility you'll get.

How to cope: Most of the time, this is a good thing. The more responsibility you have, the more skills you'll develop. This only becomes a problem if the team is getting burned out or overloaded. Under these circumstances the correct response is, "We're flattered that you think we're ready for (insert assignment), but we can't take it on right now. Let's work on juggling our current projects so we can do justice to (see previous). Is it OK if we get back to you by (some specific date)?"

Side Effect #3: Envy from Other Teams

Ironically, Side Effect #1 causes Side Effect #3 (envy).

How to cope: An easy way to spread visibility and head off envy is to share or redistribute opportunities to showcase team results. For instance, when someone asks your team to speak at a conference, you can suggest other teams that might be interested and ready for the assignment. Sometimes people in the organization get in a rut, and it's easier to ask a team they're familiar with (in this case, yours). You can help the organization become familiar with other teams' capabilities. One way to do this might be to rotate these "showcase" opportunities among all the teams, as appropriate.

Celebrating Progress; Staying Fresh and Focused

Notes. . .

Celebrate!

As you and the team become increasingly self-directed, one of the things you'll enjoy taking responsibility for is recognizing and celebrating your accomplishments. The evolution to celebrating your achievements probably parallels the reward system of your youth: At first you were praised during every step of your progress; later, teachers or coaches supplied the needed encouragement. But eventually, you were on your own and had to reward yourself: Pizza and beer for completing your tax forms, a fishing trip after a grueling home-repair project or a shopping spree for losing 20 pounds.

At this stage in your team's development, there are lots of things to celebrate. Use the chart on the next page to spark ideas about how to celebrate your team's accomplishments.

Celebrate	Examples	Your Team's Accomplishments
Team Results • Achieving a goal. • Hitting a milestone that will enable you to achieve a goal. • Improving upon last year's performance.	• Hitting service delivery targets three months in a row. • A leap of 15 percent beyond first quarter projections. • A 25 percent improvement in first-time yield over last year.	
Technical Improvements • Completing a problem-solving project. • Getting approval to implement a process improvement.	• Solution to scanner downtime implemented and working. • Got approval for purchase of new press.	
Team Development • Completing training or reaching a certification milestone. • Carrying out major new responsibilities.	• Team members 100 percent cross-trained. • First budget submitted and approved.	
External Recognition • Receiving positive feedback from a customer. • Receiving external awards or recognition.	• Letter from top customer pledging more business. • Team recognized in company newsletter for designing new tracking system.	

Celebration Do's and Don'ts

Once you've identified what to celebrate, you'll need to agree on how you'll do it. Keep the following guidelines in mind when planning team celebrations:

- The reason for the celebration should be clearly stated and understood. Don't throw a party just for the sake of having one.

- Don't hold a celebration that will intentionally antagonize or embarrass other teams. Avoid celebrating because your team has "beaten" other teams.

Here are a few suggestions for planning your celebrations. Check those that you might plan to use.

☐ Arrange for the team to present its accomplishments at a management meeting.

☐ Have a top leader treat the team to lunch.

☐ Hold a Team Appreciation Day where all the teams in your organization give brief accounts of their accomplishments.

☐ Plan a team outing (bowling, rafting, etc.).

☐ Treat the team to a baseball game or other sporting event.

☐ Have a conference room named after the team.

☐ Display the team's work in a prominent place (reception area, lunchroom, etc.).

☐ Give out VIP passes to all team members for a week—entitling them to free lunches and soft drinks in the cafeteria.

Staying Fresh and Focused

Now that you've gotten the hang of this celebration business (working in a team does have its rewards), your journey is almost complete. But there is something more for your team to learn. How do you maintain your team's freshness and sense of purpose over the coming months (and years)? It's your choice.

Staying Fresh

To keep your perspective fresh, your team might want to try some techniques that have worked for other teams. From the following list check the techniques you might want to use.

☐ **Bring in "fresh blood."** Trade team members with another team for a period of time or import a special expert for several team meetings. It's amazing how everyone's behavior changes when there's a newcomer in the group.

☐ **Rotate roles.** If you've fallen into the rut of always doing the same tasks in preparation for your meetings, switch responsibilities with someone else (even if you think you won't like the new task as much or that the other person won't handle your former task as well as you). Doing new things will keep you alert and give you a fresh perspective. Above all else, you want to avoid sleepwalking through your team responsibilities.

☐ **Learn something new as a team.** Target an area that is a team weakness (computers? contracts? sales? budgets?) and arrange for training as a group.

☐ **Take your work—but not yourselves— seriously.** Use humor to lighten up the team. Gag prizes, roasts of team members, "dress down" days, and "dubious achievement" awards all can make the team experience more fun.

☐ **Learn from other teams.** Make it a practice to implement at least one new "best practice" from another team (inside or outside your company) once a month. The teams at greatest risk of getting stale are those that don't join other teams up on deck to exchange ideas.

☐ **Invite a trainer, facilitator, or leader from another area to observe your team.** They often can point out bad habits, ruts, and blind spots that your team isn't aware of. Some teams exchange this kind of "audit" service with other teams. Some even make a game in which one team gets points for each improvement suggestion made to the other team. These points then can be traded in for future services.

☐ **Benchmark.** Send team members to conferences or other companies in your industry.

☐ **Exchange honest feedback.** Nothing jump-starts a team faster than members getting direct, specific feedback on their own behaviors.

☐ **Offer to train other teams in something that your team does well.** Not only will this help you get some recognition, it will help you be more aware of your strengths.

Staying Focused

Not sure if your team is having a difficult time keeping its focus? If you've been experiencing any of the symptoms below, focus might be a problem. Check those that might apply to your team.

☐ Leaving a team meeting without reaching agreement on tasks.

☐ Hitting a plateau of performance results.

☐ Straying from the original purpose in your charter.

☐ Deploying members to numerous, diverse tasks that are difficult to track.

☐ Spending time working on tasks when your leader directs you to work on something else.

☐ Dividing into "camps" or subgroups that want to work on "unsanctioned" projects that conflict with or strain the team's resources.

If you checked one or more of these symptoms, your team might be having a problem keeping its focus. This is not uncommon, especially when the team has the motivation and opportunity to work on a number of other interesting ideas. At the same time, you probably don't have the time or energy to waste on unnecessary tasks. Here are some suggestions your team might want to use to regain focus. Check those that you might want to try.

☐ Review (and update) your team charter at least once a quarter.

☐ At least once every six months, invite a senior manager to a team meeting to discuss the company's direction and how your team fits in.

☐ Invite customers to discuss how their requirements are changing and how your team's products or services fit in.

☐ Ask someone from the sales group in your company to talk about changing marketplace requirements.

☐ At least once a month, review team performance against established goals.

☐ Schedule a "spring cleaning" in which you go through the "team closet" and clean out non-value-adding activities that have accumulated in the past year.

☐ Renew commitment to the team by revamping your team's charter and ground rules.

One way to use these tips, tricks, and techniques is to throw them a team grab bag. Whenever the team is feeling burned out, stalled, or is otherwise suffering from general malaise, one member reaches into the grab bag and is responsible for implementing the idea he or she pulls out.

Development Activity: Repacking Your Bags

Introduction

When you started out as a team, you completed an activity to rid yourselves of old "baggage." Since then, you undoubtedly have picked up new habits that are weighing you down. It's always a good idea to take a periodic inventory of personal behaviors and habits—tossing out what isn't working anymore and taking on more productive, functional behaviors.

Each team member will leave this activity with a "bag" of positive behaviors that he or she can concentrate on.

Materials

You'll need one paper bag for each team member and a supply of 3" x 5" cards.

Total Time Allotment

90 minutes

Instructions

1. Explain that the team has come a long way and accomplished a great deal. The way to keep improving is by continuing to focus on strengths and positive behaviors.

2. Distribute 3" x 5" cards and a paper bag to each team member. (The number of cards distributed to each member should equal one more than the number of people on the team.)

3. For each team member in turn, have the remaining team members make a note on a 3" x 5" card completing this statement:

   The contribution you make to this team that I appreciate the most is . . .

   Explain that each answer must be:

   - **Specific:** "You always keep others informed about activities that might interest them" is better than "You are the glue that keeps us together."

- **Unique:** It should be something that doesn't apply to everyone on the team. ("You show up every day" or "You know all the jobs on the team" won't be very meaningful if it applies to everybody.)

4. Once everyone has completed a card for each team member, they can deposit it in the appropriate team member's bag.

5. Instruct everyone to review the cards in their bag. Then each team member should summarize the feedback and tell the group: "What you seem to appreciate is . . ."

6. Using the positive feedback as a cushion, team members should consider their own behavior and identify:

- One of their own ineffective habits or behaviors that is impeding the team.

- One new, effective behavior they would like to adopt.

Have team members write each behavior on a separate 3" x 5" card (each member should have two blank cards).

7. Going around the room in turn, have each team member reveal his or her ineffective behavior (symbolically tearing up the card) and the new, effective behavior he or she plans to adopt (dropping that card into the bag).

By the end of this activity, each team member will have a bagful of behaviors that will provide personal and team benefits. And because everyone will have heard which behaviors other team members will be trying to stop and start, they'll be able to provide support and reinforcement.

Other Sources of Help

Books About Teams

Empowered Teams (Wellins, R.S., Byham, W.C., & Wilson, J.M.; San Francisco: Jossey-Bass, 1991; 258 pp.) outlines how to implement self-directed teams successfully. It explains how self-directed teams work, how they're different from other teams, and what they do on a day-to-day basis. It covers the key factors for successful implementation taken from a variety of companies—private and public, large and small—that are using self-directed work teams. Most of all, it provides practical hands-on advice for working through the stages of building strong teams.

Inside Teams (Wellins, R.S., Byham, W.C., & Dixon, G.R.; San Francisco: Jossey-Bass, 1994; 390 pp.) offers a behind-the-scenes look at how 20 of the world's best team-based companies realized results through teamwork. Each case history chronicles why teams were chosen as a competitive strategy, how teams started, the problems encountered, the lessons learned, and the dramatic impact teams had on the organization's bottom line.

Succeeding as a Self-directed Work Team (Harper, B. & Harper, A.; Croton-on-Hudson, NY: MW Corporation, 1989; 103 pp.) asks and answers 20 common questions about teams. It is a good introduction to the concept and is presented in an easy-to-read format. The book answers questions of interest to team members (for instance, What are the benefits for team members? and, Can anyone learn to be an effective team member?) and leaders (for instance, How is leadership handled by the SDWT? and, What is the new role of the manager and supervisor?).

Succeeding With Teams (Wellins, R.S., Schaaf, D., & Shomo, K.H.; Minneapolis: Lakewood Books, 1994; 126 pp.) is a handbook for teams at all stages of development. Each chapter offers 10 tips with explanations, suggestions, and, in some cases, applications of how they've worked for other organizations.

Research Studies

Barry Macy completed a large-scale analysis of more than 130 organizations with employee involvement efforts titled "Organizational Design and Work Innovations: Impacts 1961-1991." It was published in Research in Organizational Change and Development (Vol. VII, Woodman, R.W., and Pasmore, W.A., eds., JAI Press, 1993).

John Cotter conducted a similar survey of organizations that moved to teams in seven countries, which appeared as "Designing Organizations that Work: An Open Socio-technical Systems Perspective." Copies of the study can be obtained from John J. Cotter Associates in Studio City, California.

In "Creating High-Performance Organizations: Practices and results of employee involvement and total quality management in Fortune 1000 companies" (Jossey-Bass, 1995), Edward Lawler, Susan Mohrman, and Gerald Ledford offer the most up-to-date results from a unique longitudinal study that has systematically researched the adoption and impact of employee involvement and total quality management practices on the largest companies in the United States.

About Development Dimensions International

Development Dimensions International, Inc. (DDI), is a world leader in human resource services that help organizations raise the performance of their employees and teams.

The worldwide network of teams consultants at DDI knows how to overcome the barriers that organizations face when they move to teams or seek to improve existing teams. DDI consultants have worked with more than 2,000 organizations worldwide, in businesses ranging from heavy industry to health care, helping teams achieve results like these:

- A chemicals plant reduced costs by 10 percent ($3 million).

- A radio repair facility tripled its output.

- An insurance company reduced its claims backlog from 18,000 to zero.

- A manufacturer reduced cycle time by 75 percent.

DDI's teams consultants understand the nuances of teamwork, team development, and team management. They help organizations develop and maintain highly productive teams by assessing readiness for teams, guiding work redesign, training all levels of personnel, and creating an organizational culture that is conducive to team success.

DDI's integrated human resource systems, consulting services, and support tools also help organizations build customer focus, reduce turnover, merge corporate cultures, create a new work environment, and develop a world-class workforce. Many of the world's most successful companies choose DDI to help mold their culture and develop their people. Since 1970 DDI has worked with more than 16,000 client organizations around the world, including 400 of the *Fortune* 500. Our programs have been translated into 19 languages.

For more information, write or call:

Development Dimensions International
World Headquarters—Pittsburgh
1225 Washington Pike
Bridgeville, PA 15017-2838
1-800-933-4463
World Wide Web: http://www.ddiworld.com

About the Authors

Jill George and Jeanne Wilson live, eat, and breathe teams. They are coauthors of the *Team Leader's Survival Guide* (DDI Press, 1995) and *Leadership Trapeze* (Jossey-Bass, 1994, with Richard S. Wellins and William C. Byham).

Jill and Jeanne forged DDI's teams practice, working with clients on team visioning, work redesign, leader assessment and development, and team performance management. Some of their projects included:

- Implementing self-directed teams of sales and service professionals for Buick.

- Redesigning the work flow and team boundaries at UCAR Carbon's R&D facility.

- Developing a joint union-management team implementation at several sites within Union Pacific Railroad.

- Designing a team performance management system with Miller Brewing.

- Starting up a new team-based financial services center with Unisys.

Jill has managed large-scale culture change and team implementations for DDI's multisite clients. She has achieved results by using sociotechnical systems-driven vision, design, role clarity, and team performance management interventions. Jill also has assisted in the development of DDI's team training systems, which deliver the skills needed to operate effectively in a team environment. Jill's experiences with work teams have been published in *Teams, Total Quality Management, Training & Development, and The Journal for Quality and Participation*. She received her M.S. and Ph.D. degrees in industrial/organizational psychology, both from the University of Tennessee.

Jeanne has led groups in redesigning entire operations for teams, assessing team members and leaders against the new criteria for success in a high-involvement culture, and planning new plant start-ups. Her ideas about teams have appeared in journals such as *IndustryWeek, Fortune, Total Quality Management*, and *The Journal for Quality and Participation*. Jeanne received her M.S. degree in industrial/organizational psychology from Purdue University. Currently she is pursuing her doctorate in organizational behavior at Carnegie Mellon University.

Index

We Couldn't Have Done It Without You . . .

We would like to thank the people who helped us take this guide from an idea to a finished, (we hope) fun-to-use piece.

- Once again, Bill Byham and Rich Wellins encouraged us and believed in our "idear" (usually pronounced eye-dee-uh).

- Bill Proudfoot and Mike Moore mastered the arts of tag team editing and nautical analogies.

- David Biber—who outdid himself—created the delightful cartoons and illustrations.

- Richard Hunter—who thought the editors would never stop making revisions—formatted the book and created the tables.

- Shawn Garry and Leslie Patterson each proofread the entire guide and developed two pairs of bloodshot eyes for their contributions.

- Anne Maers helped to keep afloat the idea for our little sequel to the *Team Leader's Survival Guide.*

- As we reached the deadline crunch and revisions threatened to capsize our team's boat, Deborah Freeman and Holly White came on board to help bail us out.